T0163341

Jesse Benton Frémont

Project Sponsors

Missouri Center for the Book
Western Historical Manuscript Collection,
    University of Missouri–Columbia

Special Thanks

Emily Troxell Jaycox, librarian,
    Missouri Historical Society
Christine Montgomery, photo specialist,
    State Historical Society of Missouri, Columbia
Sandy Nozick, reference librarian,
    Beale Memorial Library, Kern County Library
Emily D. Rohlfs, library clerk,
    State Historical Society of Missouri, Columbia
Adam Beck
Holly Gray
Jack Johnston
Ellen Lanto
Hallie Stone

MISSOURI HERITAGE READERS
General Editor, Rebecca B. Schroeder

Each Missouri Heritage Reader explores a particular aspect of the state's rich cultural heritage. Focusing on people, places, historical events, and the details of daily life, these books illustrate the ways in which people from all parts of the world contributed to the development of the state and the region. The books incorporate documentary and oral history, folklore, and informal literature in a way that makes these resources accessible to all Missourians.

Intended primarily for adult new readers, these books will also be invaluable to readers of all ages interested in the cultural and social history of Missouri.

Other Books in the Series

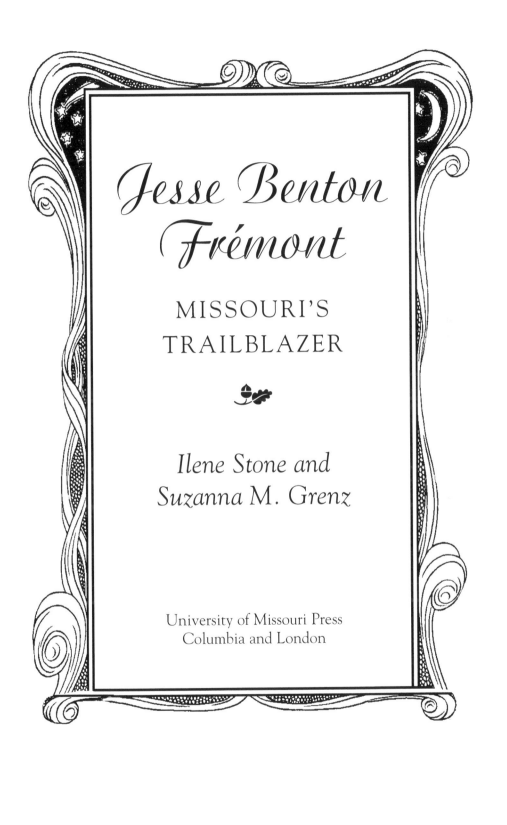

Jesse Benton Frémont

MISSOURI'S TRAILBLAZER

Ilene Stone and Suzanna M. Grenz

University of Missouri Press
Columbia and London

Copyright © 2005 by
The Curators of the University of Missouri
University of Missouri Press, Columbia, Missouri 65201
Printed and bound in the United States of America

5 4 3 2 1   09 08 07 06 05

Library of Congress Cataloging-in-Publication Data

Stone, Ilene, 1945–
Jessie Benton Frémont, Missouri's trailblazer / Ilene Stone and Suzanna
M. Grenz.
p. cm. — (Missouri heritage readers)
Includes bibliographical references (p.) and index.
ISBN-13: 978-0-8262-1628-1
ISBN-10: 0-8262-1628-5 (alk. paper)
1. Frémont, Jessie Benton, 1824–1902. 2. Politicians' spouses—United
States—Biography. 3. Frémont, John Charles, 1813–1890—Marriage. 4.
Women pioneers—West (U.S.)—Biography. 5. Women pioneers—Missouri—
Biography. 6. Women—Missouri—Biography. 7. Missouri—Biography. I.
Title: Jessie Benton Frémont. II. Grenz, Suzanna M. III. Title. IV. Series.
E415.9.F79S86 2005
973.6092—dc22
2005052991

⊗™ This paper meets the requirements of the
American National Standard for Permanence of Paper
for Printed Library Materials, Z39.48, 1984.

Designer: Stephanie Foley
Typesetter: Foley Design
Printer and binder: Thomson-Shore, Inc.
Typefaces: Ariston BQ, Goudy and NeutraText

Publication of this book has been generously assisted
by a contribution from Sprint Foundation.

To the staff of the James S. Copley Library

Carol, Ron, and Harold,
without you and your friendship
our Jessie would not have come to life

Contents

Preface

*O*ver the years many authors have written books and articles about Jessie Benton Frémont. She was the daughter of the famous United States senator from Missouri, Thomas Hart Benton, and the wife of famed western explorer John Charles Frémont. The works about Jessie come from varying points of view—from the historical fiction of Irving Stone's *Immortal Wife* (1944) to the serious historical work of Pamela Herr's *Jessie Benton Frémont: A Biography* (1987). Our book, *Jessie Benton Frémont: Missouri's Trailblazer,* falls in between, because our purpose is to provide a book that is based on extensive research yet at the same time appeals to the general reader.

Initially, we wanted to disengage Jessie from her father and her husband; we wanted to bring her out from under their historical influence, making her stand apart from them, to stand by herself. This was difficult because Jessie's life was so intertwined with those two very important men. Nevertheless, by concentrating on the broad picture, we focused on pivotal events in her life and found that, in this way, Jessie did emerge as herself—a person of strength, determination, and conviction. Our work resulted in a portrait of an exceptional woman. Jessie was someone who challenged the norms of her day and by doing so found a place not only in the history of Missouri but in her adopted state of California as well. Both states can be proud to claim her as one of their own.

In putting together this most recent biography of Jessie Benton Frémont, we relied on primary sources such as Jessie's own accounts of various important events in her life, including her trek across the Panamanian Isthmus, the essential role she played in her husband's career, and the emergence of her own prominence, to mention a few. Also utilized were her daughter Elizabeth's book and John Charles Frémont's writings. We also gave proper attention to important secondary materials. Our research led us to the writings of prominent American historians and others who distinguished themselves on this subject.

In no way do we consider our work as the ultimate or definitive biography of Jessie Benton Frémont. However, the account of her life as told in this book will reflect who she was, what she stood for, how she strove to achieve what she believed in, and how she sacrificed to make her ideas a reality. We think it is a good story and hope that those who read it will enjoy it.

Acknowledgments

*A*n endeavor such as this begins with a great deal of hope, continues with an enormous amount of work, and ends with a large measure of appreciation for all the assistance provided along the way. Thus, there are numerous people who contributed to this effort and it is essential to properly thank them.

Of all of the marvelous individuals who gave advice and guidance, none deserves recognition more than Becky Schroeder, general editor of the Missouri Heritage Readers Series. This is my second collaboration with her, and I am more in awe than ever of her knowledge of all things literary, her grammar skills, and most of all her personal patience, which is calming and soothing to a writer who at times is overwhelmed. Becky is so very good at what she does: helping turn preliminary manuscripts into completed books that are readable. She is a treasure and as proud as I am to have her as my editor, I cherish our friendship even more. There is another person in the Schroeder household I must thank—Becky's husband, Dolf. Each and every time I called Becky and Dolf answered the phone, he greeted me with a warm response and made my intrusion seem welcome, which I so appreciated.

I would especially like to thank Dr. Lawrence O. Christensen, professor emeritus at the University of Missouri–Rolla, for his contributions to this work. This was my third time working with Dr. Christensen, and each time it has been a delight. As in the past, his ideas were invaluable; his recommendations and suggestions only enhanced the manuscript and made it more complete. I so value all of his input and evaluation; that he would take time to work on this project is an honor.

Once more Gary Kass was my editor at the University of Missouri Press. His work on behalf of all of the manuscripts he oversees makes them so much better. This is certainly true of this work, and again it was a true pleasure to cooperate with him to bring this project to publication.

This book is dedicated to the staff of the James S. Copley Library in La Jolla, California, and it must be stated what an absolutely wonderful place it is to visit and to do research. Not many collections greet a patron with a cup of coffee in the morning; not many facilities are designed to resemble a personal library; not many provide an environment where the researcher's needs are always paramount and the staff does everything it can do to fulfill your immediate requests. Without the assistance of Carol Beales, the manager of the library, Ronald Vanderhye, assistant registrar, and Harold Koplke, conservator, it is hard to imagine this book ever being completed. They are professionals in every way. The materials at the Copley on the Frémonts, both primary and secondary, are extraordinary for a small, private facility; this made research there most enjoyable.

The staffs at the Huntington Library in San Marino, California, the Bancroft Library at the University of California, Berkeley, and the Arizona State Library, Archives and Public Records, in Phoenix, Arizona, were more than helpful in making available the items from their vast collections that were necessary for this project. Their contributions made this book more accurate and complete.

Doing research from California was not easy and often I needed to contact people in Missouri for information. I am indebted to those who work at the State Historical Society of Missouri in Columbia and the Missouri Historical Society in St. Louis. No matter when I phoned or who I talked to, they were always kind, considerate, and helpful—traits that a researcher, especially one doing long-distance investigations, most appreciates. The people at the Western Historical Manuscript Collection–Columbia and the Boone County Historical Society, Columbia, made my initial research easier. When I first started the process of gathering information on Jessie Benton Frémont, these individuals offered their guidance and advice, and I am grateful for their support.

Closer to home, two librarians at Palomar College in San Marcos, California, deserve special kudos. Anytime I needed a book, a map, or any other item, Denise Brown and Mary Russell were there to help. They made tracking down bits of information so much easier. It was nice to be able to rely upon them.

In the end, I must thank my husband, Jeff, who was my "unofficial" editor, reading chapters and the entire manuscript when needed. He is also my biggest cheerleader, and for that I am most thankful. There are other family members and friends who lent encouragement to this project, and I feel deep gratitude for their support. However, despite all the guidance of so many people, any errors, mistakes, or omissions belong to me and Sue alone. With all of this said, it was a pleasure to write about Jessie Benton Frémont and pass along some new insights into who she was—a Missouri trailblazer.

I.S.

Jesse Benton Frémont

CHAPTER 1

The Bentons

*J*essie Ann Benton was the daughter of Sen. Thomas Hart Benton, but in his mind, and perhaps in hers too, she was the son the senator wanted. She was born into a family of status and privilege, two things she would strive her whole life to attain in her own right, with mixed success. Her life was crowded and exciting; she traveled to, and lived in, exotic places that most people never visited, let alone a proper nineteenth-century woman. She met important people from all walks of life, including several presidents of the United States, one of whom she passionately argued with—something people of any century rarely do. At times her situation bordered on near poverty, and she ended her years living quietly—not in Missouri, but in the soon-to-be megalopolis of Los Angeles, California—writing about and defending the memory of the husband to whom she devoted her life. Her ashes are buried in upstate New York in a family plot overlooking the Hudson River, the final resting place after a remarkable life journey.

It all began on May 31, 1824, when Jessie was born on her mother's family estate, Cherry Grove, which is nestled in the Blue Ridge Mountains of Virginia in Rockbridge County, near Lexington. Her mother, Elizabeth Preston McDowell, had married Thomas Hart Benton in 1821 at the age of twenty-six, after a long courtship.

Elizabeth, the youngest of three children, came from a long line of famous Virginians that included senators, congressmen, governors, and other state officeholders. According to Pamela

Herr, author of *Jessie Benton Frémont: A Biography*, Elizabeth's "upbringing combined the ease and grace of upper-class southern life" with a religious background rooted in Presbyterianism. Jessie once wrote that her mother was spoiled "in every way." Elizabeth's days were typical of a sheltered southern belle: there were winter residences, summer homes, galas, concerts, dinners, and balls. Her education was characteristic of women of her era and standing; in addition to reading and writing, she learned the social skills necessary to meet the obligations of her position in southern society. Jessie wrote in *Souvenirs of My Time* that her mother had a "genius for home comfort" that allowed her to guide her household with ease.

Thomas Hart Benton was already a U.S. senator from Missouri when he married Elizabeth. Fearful of his affinity for the American West, she accepted his marriage proposal only after a six-year delay, waiting until his election to national office made his life appear more stable. He was almost forty when he and Elizabeth wed at Cherry Grove in March 1821. The newly-weds honeymooned in St. Louis, where he busied himself with political affairs and she became acquainted with the city that was the gateway to the American West. Elizabeth never really accepted the rough-and-tumble of frontier Missouri and always considered Cherry Grove her proper home.

Benton was born on March 14, 1782, in Hillsborough, North Carolina. His father's name was Jesse and he later chose that name for his second daughter. When Benton was eight, his father died, falling victim to the family nemesis of tuberculosis. He left behind eight children, including his third child and first son, Thomas. If his father had lived, Thomas Hart Benton would have been a member of the gentry class, but he found himself instead in different circumstances. His widowed mother, Ann, found ways to provide for her family, even saving enough money to send Thomas to the new college at Chapel Hill in North Carolina. Financial problems arose, though, and after allega-tions of theft, the university expelled him. Humiliated, but a proud man, Benton from that time on dedicated himself to

This portrait of Sen. Thomas Hart Benton appeared in *Thirty Years' View*, the book he wrote about his long and distinguished career in public service. (James S. Copley Library, La Jolla, California)

achieving a reputation for honest integrity. He went to seek his future in Tennessee, where his mother and siblings had already settled. Not wanting a farm life, Benton studied law and before long entered Tennessee politics. He met Andrew Jackson and the two became allies, drawn together by their common vision of westward expansion, which they believed was the key to America's future. After some time, the two men had a serious disagreement and shared some heated exchanges over Jackson's insults of Benton's brother, Jesse. The animosity led to a famous brawl in 1813, which included a duel. No one was killed, but Benton wounded Jackson. Two years later, at the age of thirty-

Lithograph showing the St. Louis skyline in 1840, a view that would have been very familiar to Jessie. (State Historical Society of Missouri, Columbia)

three, Benton left Tennessee for the Missouri Territory. It would take years for Benton and Jackson to heal their rift.

In St. Louis, Benton became a successful attorney, the editor of the *St. Louis Enquirer*, and a skilled politician. Using the newspaper to promote his ideas on Missouri statehood and the right of any state to decide the slavery issue for itself, Benton became a contender for the U.S. Senate after Missouri entered the Union in 1821 as a slave state. Indeed, in that year he was chosen by the state legislature to be one of Missouri's first two senators. He was a Democrat. Eventually he would serve five terms, becoming the first U.S. senator to achieve that distinction. It was shortly after his first election that he married Elizabeth McDowell and started a family.

The Bentons had seven children: four girls and two boys survived childbirth and one child was stillborn. Of all his children, the second one, Jessie Ann, was Benton's dearest. As Jessie wrote in *A Year of American Travel*: "He made me a companion and a friend from the time almost that I could begin to understand. We were a succession of girls at first, with the boys coming last, and my father gave me early the place a son would have had; and my perfect health—without a flaw until I was twenty-four—gave me not only the good spirits but the endurance and application that pleased him."

Any disappointment that Jessie was not the son Benton wanted—he had already picked the name Thomas—disappeared quickly, and he shaped his second child into the person she became: an individual who would do him proud and bring honor to the Benton name. Jessie's choice of a husband, however, would test her father's faith in his daughter.

CHAPTER 2

Jessie Meets John

In 1830, Washington, D.C., was a city of about twenty thousand people and the capital of a rapidly developing nation. Fortunately for Thomas, Elizabeth, and their five children—Elizabeth (Eliza), Jessie, Randolph, Sarah, and Susan—they lived in a brick house that was generous enough to accommodate their large family and the many servants needed to run such a household. In truth, the Bentons had three homes, as Jessie wrote in *Year*: "the winter home in Washington, which was 'ours'; that in St. Louis, which was 'our father's home'; and that of our grandfather in Virginia, which was my mother's dearly loved home, and my birthplace as well as hers." Over the years the family spent time in all three, but it was the home in St. Louis that prepared Jessie for her life on the frontier. As she wrote:

> From the broad gallery of my father's house in St. Louis there was always to be seen in my earlier days a kaleidoscopic variety of figures; the lower class of French . . . long files of Indians stepping silently by, the squaws and babies bringing up the rear—real Indians in real Indian dress . . . any number of clergy; hunters and trappers in fringed deerskins; army officers in worn uniforms going by on horseback.

Missouri was still very much a primitive, western region, and St. Louis had a distinctive French quality. This is not surprising, since Missouri was part of the Louisiana Territory that had belonged to France only a few decades earlier. Jessie, describing the city in several of her writings, wrote that houses often were built in the French manner, with large garden courtyards; the French language was prevalent; and some French social customs were observed. "Growing up in its midst," she wrote of St. Louis, "I felt at home in all French domestic ideas when I lived in France."

Jessie's life was not always idyllic, and at times reality intruded. At age eight, while visiting St. Louis, she witnessed an outbreak of cholera that struck the frontier city. The epidemic was traumatic for adults, but especially so for the children. She described what happened in *Souvenirs*: "At first we were only told we were not to go to school. Then, we were to play only with each other in our own grounds and no more little friends visited us or we them. The friends who came to my father on the long gallery were as many as ever, but they and he himself no longer had any pleasant leisure, but were quick and busy in coming and going and all looked grave."

Those people that could escape St. Louis did so, seeking safety from the disease. The Benton family did not. They stayed. Jessie continued: "In this condition of universal alarm, when nearly all who could, fled from the town, even clergymen deserting their churches, my father thought it right for him to stay and give the encouragement and example of his presence. With his courage and sense of duty this was easy, but it must have been hard to him to risk my mother and all of us children." Not only did the Bentons remain in the stricken city, but their house became a "'diet kitchen;' good soups, preparations of rice, and well-filtered and purified water . . . became the occupation of the house." Decontaminated water was essential during this time of infection, and children like Jessie became involved in making the drinking water clean:

All the water was brought in large barrels from the river and poured bucket by bucket, into great jars of red earthenware, some of them five feet high. These jars had their own large cool room paved with glazed red brick and level with the street. The jars of drinking water and for cooking were clarified of the mud of the river by alum and blanched almonds, and then filtered. So much was needed now that even we children were useful in this sort of work.

It was a difficult time. The Bentons fortunately avoided the fate of many who fell victim to the cholera epidemic; even though Jessie's mother and a devoted servant did become ill, both eventually recovered.

Jessie's trips to her ancestral homes had a profound effect on her, as she reflected years later when she wrote the dedication to her husband's book *Memoirs of My Life*: "I was bred up in the 'religion of the hearth' and the obligation, and I really think the affection of 'kinsmen.'" Jessie thus developed a true affinity for things beyond the establishment. She continued, "My mother was rather pitied for her transplanting to the 'West' and she herself had a mild contempt for our house in Washington, because it was bought and not inherited." Jessie grew up more open, more accepting of new ideas and places, more egalitarian—more like her senator father than her aristocratic mother.

According to Catherine Coffin Phillips's *Jessie Benton Frémont: The Woman Who Made History*, "Jessie was a healthy little girl of five, with red-brown curls, brown eyes, and delicately tinted oval features which already foretold of her beauty." With her mother attending to the older, but frail, Eliza and the younger children, Jessie was left on her own a good deal of the time. Hence, she found her way to her father. Phillips states: "To her father she was from the first an enchanting but exasperating child, with dynamic quality, a will to do something about it, a force and fearlessness which marked her as his own. He realized that such personality must express itself and that certain salient characteristics, even now emerging, must be developed under strong and steady guidance." Thus, the lifelong special relationship between Jessie and her father began. As Jessie wrote in *Souvenirs*, "I think I came into my father's life by a breath of his

Miniature portrait of young Jessie. (Frémont Letters and Papers, James S. Copley Library)

own compelling nature; strong, resolute, but open to all tender and gracious influences."

Benton saw to it that his children received the education expected of his class and position. He wanted to give all of his children quality instruction—this included home schooling, at times from his wife, and at times from him. It also meant that Eliza and Jessie attended a French school when the family was in St. Louis. And of course, there were tutors teaching a variety of subjects. Jessie, however, received extra attention from her father. He taught her from his own vast collection of books. In her writings Jessie recalled, "[A]t all times I had the right . . . to go to my father's library, where walls of books rose to the ceiling on every side." There was always a spot for Jessie in her father's library, usually near the fireplace. In addition, when Senator Benton visited the White House to attend a meeting with the president, Jessie frequently tagged along. When her father went to his Capitol office, Jessie often went with him. Sometimes he dropped her off at the Library of Congress, the core of which came from Thomas Jefferson's library. The staff of the library allowed Jessie to browse through the volumes at her own pace. As Jessie entered her teens, however, a change came in her schooling—there would be fewer tutors, less special attention from her father, less privileged browsing of the shelves of literary collections, and more structure to her education.

In 1838, when Jessie was fourteen, she and Eliza entered Georgetown's premier girl's boarding school: Miss English's Female Seminary. The reason for their enrollment was to keep suitors away. Jessie had already received several marriage proposals, but her parents thought her much too young for marriage—and they thought the same for delicate Eliza, who required particular attention to keep her healthy. Jessie was unhappy with the decision. Pamela Herr writes that Jessie "despised the school. She found that the democratic ideals she had absorbed from her father and from her long stays in frontier St. Louis were at odds with this 'society in miniature,' where rank and wealth dominated even on the playground." Her misery, though, was soon tempered when she met the man she would marry—John Charles Frémont.

Frémont's family background was not what Thomas and Elizabeth Benton had in mind for their daughter. A child of a tempestuous relationship, Frémont was born on January 21, 1813, to Anne Beverley Whiting Pryor and Charles Frémon. His mother was "a spirited and beautiful young woman, the picture of animation and energy," according to Allan Nevins, author of *Frémont: Pathmarker of the West*. In 1796 she married Maj. John Pryor, an American Revolutionary War veteran from the Tidewater area of Virginia, near Richmond. The marriage was a rocky one from the beginning and Anne soon strayed. Nevins writes that Anne, "tired of her fast-ageing husband, became acquainted with a handsome French émigré Charles Frémon . . . a dark, slender man, with fine features [and] manners." Frémon, who made his way in the world by teaching French, fascinated Anne. With no children from her marriage to Pryor, and feeling that time was slipping away, she pursued Frémon. Nevins gives a vivid account of what followed: "Early in 1811, the inevitable explosion occurred. In the presence of Frémon . . . the enraged husband taxed Mrs. Pryor with flagrant misconduct and even threatened to erase the blot on his honor by killing her. She drew her self up, blazing with anger, and told him: 'You may spare yourself the crime. I shall leave your house to-morrow morning forever!'"

Frémon wanted to attack Pryor, but instead the lovers left Richmond almost immediately, with Anne Pryor taking what she could, including her personal slaves. In those days, only the state legislature of Virginia could grant a divorce, and it eventually did that for Major Pryor, who soon remarried. But a marriage decree was not in effect for Charles and Anne when John Charles was born in Savannah, Georgia, though his parents eventually married. For practical purposes, John Charles Frémont was considered illegitimate.

Charles and Anne traveled through the South, trying to support their family, which eventually included two more children. He taught French and she toiled in a boardinghouse. Charles died in 1818, just seven years after he and Anne started their life together. Charley, as John Charles was called, was five years old. Anne took up residence in Charleston, South Carolina, where Charley grew up.

Nevins remarks that Charley had a "lively adventurous temperament" and that his mother most likely ran a boardinghouse to support her family. Herr declares that he was an "exceptionally bright and attractive boy, with gray-blue eyes, olive skin, and the natural dash of his French father." He had many friends and soon found a patron in a Charleston attorney. All of his life, John Charles Frémont skillfully acquired support from prominent men to further his career and personal goals. This benefactor secured an enrollment for him in Charleston College in 1829. Though showing great ability in mathematics, he neglected his studies and, just three months before graduation, was dismissed from school.

Needing employment, Frémont—who sometime after his father's death added a *t* to his name but kept the accent—soon found another sponsor in a trustee of Charleston College. He was Joel Robert Poinsett, a prominent American diplomat. One of his early postings was as the American ambassador to Mexico, and when he returned home he introduced a plant to the United States that became a holiday favorite—the poinsettia. Poinsett took a liking to Frémont and found him a position aboard the naval ship *Natchez,* which was soon to leave on a journey to South America. Frémont was the mathematics instructor on the boat, and not only did he find a job, but he also found his life's work: studying the frontier. His new profession also eventually led him to the person he would marry—Jessie Ann Benton.

By 1838, Frémont was a second lieutenant in the U.S. Army's Bureau of Topographical Engineers. His career led him to explorations of the Missouri and Mississippi Rivers and he became an ardent westward expansionist, which in turn brought him to the attention of influential people who held similar views. One of those people was the senator from Missouri, Thomas Hart Benton, who had a long-standing belief in the importance of manifest destiny—the conviction that it was the obvious duty of the United States to expand from the East Coast to the West. Jessie wrote in *Souvenirs:* "It became my father's fixed idea, with a growth proportioned to the greatness of the subject, that this great West must be opened to emigration, and, when possible, a good harbor secured on the Pacific. You may say *the* good harbor, for there is but the one—that of San Francisco." The relationship that the two men forged would make Jessie, as she said, "the connecting link between my father's thought, and that thought made action by Mr. Frémont." Jessie and her future husband

Photograph of John Charles Frémont. While taken years after he first met Jessie, he still looked imposing in his full-dress uniform, something that captivated her at an early age. (State Historical Society of Missouri, Columbia)

became committed to making Benton's dreams of American expansion to the Pacific Ocean a reality.

Frémont met Senator Benton in late 1839 while he was in Washington to report on his latest western expedition. A mutual friend and Frémont patron, Joel R. Poinsett, by then secretary of war, introduced the two men, knowing of their mutual interest in exploring and developing the American West. This meeting led to informal dinners at the Benton home and an invitation to Frémont to attend a concert at Miss English's school. He was Eliza's escort, but he met Jessie.

Jessie was ready for a change. According to Phillips, the school principal had reported to her father that the strong-willed girl was anything but an ideal pupil: "Miss Jessie although extremely intelligent, lacks the docility of a model student. Moreover, she has the objectionable manner of seeming to take our orders and assignments under consideration, to be accepted or disregarded by some standard of her own." And then along came the handsome army lieutenant.

By some accounts, it was love at first sight. In his *Memoirs*, Frémont remembered his first meeting with Jessie: "She was then in the bloom of her girlish beauty. Naturally I was attracted." Jessie was not yet sixteen, but, according to Nevins, Frémont was taken in not only by her beauty but also by a "vivacity, which more than matched his own; her grasp of mind, her tenacious memory and her quick perception, all inherited from her father." For her part, Jessie was equally smitten with the army officer who displayed a dynamic personality and a great passion for the West. However, it would be six months before Jessie and John saw each other again; his work took him back to exploring a portion of the frontier.

The Bentons were less than enthusiastic about their daughter's relationship with a man of doubtful ancestry and limited means. Jessie, though, saw it differently. Herr explains it this way:

Through him, the future beckoned—romantic, adventurous, alluring. Perhaps she sensed that here was a man who could cross the rivers and mountains and plains that were only words in her father's mouth. She may have dreamed that he could carry out, as she, a woman, could not, her father's vision of a nation stretching to the Pacific. Perhaps she already knew that she found a hero-worth-the-making in John Charles Frémont. It was not without reason that her perceptive and fond father had nicknamed his favorite daughter "Imagination."

So, despite disapproval from the Bentons, and in a secret ceremony, Jessie Ann Benton became Mrs. John Charles Frémont on October 19, 1841. She was just seventeen. Ultimately, her parents accepted the marriage, and Senator Benton, in particular, worked to promote the career of his favorite daughter's husband. Jessie would do things, see places, travel far and wide, meet extraordinary people, experience adventures that few men or women of any era could imagine. The journey began.

CHAPTER 3

The Frémonts ~ The Early Years

The Frémonts' time together as newlyweds was short-lived—soon John was off on a new western trip and Jessie remained at home. They were to be separated by many months and many miles, and yet the success of this exploration, and indeed of Frémont's career, was inexorably tied to Jessie.

In May 1842, Frémont left for his first expedition after his marriage. His task was to explore parts of Missouri, Kansas, and Wyoming, paying special attention to the Rocky Mountains. Helping him in this venture was Christopher "Kit" Carson, the western adventurer, guide, and trapper who was to gain fame as a scout for Frémont and others who journeyed west. Carson was born in Kentucky in 1809 and grew up near Franklin, Missouri, in the Boone's Lick region. Apprenticed to a saddlemaker at fourteen, he ran away shortly thereafter. The following announcement appeared in the *Missouri Intelligencer* on October 12, 1826: "Christopher Carson, a boy of about 16 years old, small of his age, but thick set, light hair, ran away. . . . All persons are notified not to harbor . . . or assist said boy under penalty of the law." His "owner" offered a one-cent reward for his return, but Kit had left the area to begin his lifelong adventures in the American West. Carson shared Fremont's enthusiasm for exploring the frontier and the two men teamed up for several trips, becoming professional colleagues and personal friends. When Jessie helped her husband write the accounts of his western travels, she included Carson's contributions, and the pioneer from Missouri became famous.

A young Kit Carson sat for this portrait in his scouting clothes. A guide on many of Frémont's expeditions, he was a special confidante to Jessie and they remained friends until his death on May 23, 1868. (State Historical Society of Missouri, Columbia)

When Frémont departed, he left behind a bride who was heartbroken over his going. The concern Jessie felt was complicated by the fact that she was expecting their first child. There was nothing she could do but wait. Her anxiety was heightened because another family member was also undertaking this arduous journey: her brother John Randolph Benton was in Frémont's party. In his official report on the expedition, Frémont stated that Ran, as he was called, was "a lively boy of twelve, son of the Hon. Thomas H. Benton, [and he] accompanied me for the development of mind and body which such an expedition would give." Ran traveled with the group as far west as Fort Laramie, in present-day Wyoming. Frémont considered it too risky to take him farther, into harm's way from potential Indian trouble, so Ran returned home. In the formal account of the expedition, Frémont wrote that "Randolph had been the life of

Fort Laramie, a stopping place on Frémont's 1842 western trek. It was from here that Jessie's brother Ran began his journey back east, because it was deemed too dangerous for the young man to continue traveling west. *(Memoirs of My Life,* by John Charles Frémont; James S. Copley Library)

the camp . . . [and] it was much regretted by the men, to whom his buoyant spirits had afforded great amusement," when he left the group. Ran went on to other pursuits, including honing his foreign-language skills: he spoke his hosts' language fluently when appearing before the St. Louis German community in March 1852 to welcome Hungarian nationalist Louis Kossuth to the city. Unfortunately, a few days later, Ran became ill with a malaria-type fever and died at the age of twenty-two.

To keep herself occupied while her husband and brother were trekking through America's frontier, Jessie helped her father with his work, particularly his efforts relating to western expansion, and the old intimacy they had once shared was revived. Jessie also tended to her mother, who had suffered a severe stroke. Despite all of this activity, she longed for her husband. Happiness came again when Frémont returned home on October 29. Two weeks later, on November 15, 1842, they became the parents of a healthy girl. The baby was named Elizabeth after Jessie's mother, but she would always be known as Lily. Jessie was a mother at age eighteen. Lily was the first of five children born to the Frémonts; only three would live to adulthood.

After the excitement of Frémont's safe return and the birth of Lily subsided, the work of documenting Frémont's expedition started. In many ways, it took precedence over all else. An exciting and accurate account of his travels was very important if Frémont was to gain the support necessary for future explorations of the American West. Jessie wanted to do all she could to make sure that happened, and she thus assumed the crucial role she was to play in her husband's life: she became his chief collaborator in chronicling all of his western journeys. The writing of the account of the first expedition began in the fall of 1842 and continued through the winter of 1843.

Frémont believed Jessie's contributions to be vital. He admitted in his *Memoirs* that writing was not his best talent: "I write more easily by dictation. Writing myself I have too much time to think and dwell upon words as well as ideas." So it fell to Jessie to help him. It was a task she more than welcomed, and they developed a routine to complete the report. The work took place at the Benton home in Washington, where the Frémonts were living. Frémont described it this way:

Mrs. Frémont worked with me daily. . . . Punctually at nine o'clock Mrs. Frémont joined me. From that hour until one the writing went on, with seldom any thing to break the thread; the dictation sometimes continuing for hours, interrupted only when an occasional point of exceptional interest brought out inquiry or discussion. After the four hours' stretch there was tea with a light luncheon and then a walk to the river; and after that, it was work again until dusk.

And what a job Jessie did! While the ideas and thoughts were Frémont's, "she added elegant touches and gave variety to his vocabulary," according to Allan Nevins. The report was a success and portions of it were printed in newspapers throughout the country. Thus, early on, Jessie displayed the writing talent that she would use later in the stories she wrote about her own exciting and adventurous life.

The lure of the West spread to Americans everywhere when they read the report. As for Frémont, his passion for the frontier continued and his captivation with exploration never left him. Even while he and Jessie were writing about his most recent exploits, he was making plans for a second trek that was to be one of the most ambitious explorations of the American West since Lewis and Clark's travels forty years earlier. While preparations for this trip went on, Jessie took over answering most, if not all, of Frémont's correspondence. She enjoyed being busy, believed in western expansion, and besides, as a mere lieutenant, her husband was not entitled to a secretary. So she gladly filled that position, too. Prior to Frémont's leaving to explore the Oregon Territory, the Rocky Mountains, and trails to the Pacific, the Benton and Frémont households moved to St. Louis. Jessie would live in the Benton home there and wait for her husband to return.

Frémont left St. Louis on May 13, 1843, and traveled to Kaw Landing, near present-day Kansas City, from where the expedition would leave. Once more, the parting was hard on Jessie, but she believed in her husband's work and she might also have liked the attention his expeditions attracted. Pamela Herr writes: "[S]he had savored the brief taste of glory the first journey had brought. Now she wanted the full cup." Whether this can be believed or not, Jessie certainly brought attention to herself by supporting her husband's desire for a howitzer cannon!

In addition to all the equipment and provisions needed for a long western trip, Frémont also took with him to Kaw Landing a cannon. On May 8 he had asked Col. Stephen W. Kearny for the heavy armament. Kearny was the commander of the Third Military Department located at Jefferson Barracks, not far from St. Louis. Supposedly Frémont needed the cannon for protection, but its use in those days against Indian attacks was unusual. Nevertheless, Kearny forwarded Frémont's request to the St. Louis arsenal, where it was honored without asking approval from higher military command.

This depiction of Frémont's trip west in 1843 includes an image of the infamous howitzer cannon that Frémont took with him without proper permission from military authorities. (State Historical Society of Missouri, Columbia)

Army officials disapproved of this development. The presence of a cannon gave the expedition the appearance of a hostile undertaking. This was not the purpose of the mission, nor did Washington want to give the impression that it was; it was an excursion dedicated to scientific exploration. In an 1891 magazine article, Jessie recalled what happened next: "One day there came for [Frémont] an official letter from his colonel [John J. Abert], the chief of the Topographical Bureau: it was an order recalling him to Washington, whither he was directed to return and explain why he had armed his party with a howitzer. . . . I saw at once that this would make delays which would involve the overthrow of great plans."

Having taken it upon herself to act as her husband's secretary, Jessie opened all his mail, including the envelope containing the order for Frémont to return to Washington. She interpreted the summons as an attempt to sabotage her husband's trip and perhaps his career. "[W]ithout telling any one of the order," she sent a trusted messenger to Frémont with an urgent note to begin his journey immediately. "I wrote Mr. Frémont that he *must not ask why*, but must start at once, ready or not ready."

After learning of his departure, Jessie informed Washington that her husband had already left for the West, explaining that he needed the cannon to face possible Indian hostilities. The authorities were angry and upset. There was little they could do, because by then Frémont was beyond reach—just as Jessie had planned. In a time when instant communication was not possible as it is today, there was no way to recall him. It took Jessie's influential father to smooth things out and essentially save Frémont's career.

Was Jessie correct? Was someone in the government or in military circles trying to damage her husband's position, or did she overreact? Historians and biographers of both Jessie and John differ on these points. Some believe that the entire controversy about the howitzer was created by Frémont, Jessie, and Benton to burnish Frémont's reputation. In a well-researched 1966 article titled "The Myth of the Frémont Howitzer," Donald Jackson wrote that the story "appears to have been an absolute fiction" that has made its way into American history as truth.

Jackson is somewhat harsh in his conclusion that the howitzer cannon story was a total fabrication. The fact remains that Jessie did receive a letter to Frémont from his superior, Col. John J. Abert. Noting that Frémont had requisitioned the cannon, Abert reminded him that his trek west was to be peaceful, implying that Frémont should return if he encountered danger or hostilities. Jessie, in her role as protector-in-chief of her husband, read the note as an order to cancel the expedition, a move that could put Frémont's career in jeopardy. Given Jessie's personality and drive, she was determined to do everything to prevent her husband from complying with a vague order to turn back.

Whatever the assessment of the details surrounding the cannon, historians agree that Jessie was a strong woman, operating confidently in a man's world. Jessie may have exaggerated

Abert's letter, and her overstatement caused a furor that required her powerful father to step in and back her up—an early-day spin machine went into effect. Senator Benton and the Frémonts took on the establishment, and the stakes were high: any future that Frémont hoped to have in the army, in the exploration of the West, or in contributing to the continuing manifest destiny of the United States was in the balance. In addition, they had to exonerate Jessie from any wrongdoing. Saving the reputation of his family was essential to Benton—together they formed a powerful triumvirate in their passion to promote the American western movement, thus making sure the country would stretch "from sea to shining sea." Right or wrong, Jessie played a significant role in an episode that became part of the historical lore of America's past.

It would be many long months before Jessie saw her husband again. Occasionally she heard about Frémont from traders, trappers, or Indians who encountered him on the frontier and then made their way back to St. Louis. They delivered messages from him that told her how he was and how the expedition was progressing. These reports gave her comfort, but as the months dragged on, her despair deepened. To ease her own concerns and have something to occupy her time, Jessie went to the home of a St. Louis cousin whose husband was gravely ill with tuberculosis. Frémont finally did return, but his reunion with Jessie was delayed by a bizarre series of events.

Late on the night of August 6, 1844, Frémont found his way to the junction of the Missouri and Mississippi Rivers. By the time he reached the heart of St. Louis it was very early in the morning; with no carriages available, he walked to the Benton home. For some reason, he did not go into the house, but instead awakened the coachman, who lived in the carriage house, and asked him if all of the family was well. The coachman told him they were and that Jessie was at her cousin's house. Frémont started walking there, but fatigue got the better of him and he decided to stop in a hotel. Meanwhile, the coachman hurried to Jessie to tell her about Frémont's return. She did not believe

During his explorations, Frémont did not carry an official United States flag with him. However, he did take a pennant made for him by Jessie. Like the traditional flag, it had thirteen red and white stripes. A blue eagle clutching arrows and a peace pipe is surrounded by twenty-six stars, indicating that the pennant was made sometime between 1837, when Michigan was admitted to the Union as the twenty-sixth state, and 1845, when Florida became the twenty-seventh state. *(Memoirs of My Life,* James S. Copley Library)

him—she thought he had seen a ghost! The mystery was solved in the morning when Frémont made his way to Jessie and they were reunited, ending an extremely long separation.

Jessie and her husband stayed in St. Louis for only two weeks before hurrying back to her parents' house in the nation's capital. Once there, they collaborated on the report of Frémont's latest westward adventure, settling into the same routine they had established in the past: Frémont dictated while Jessie wrote, bringing her stylistic phrasing to his thoughts. As before, while they worked, preparations began for a third mission. This trip would be different. Tension between Mexico and the United

States over the growing American interest in the far west was increasing. The impending expedition included a venture into California, from where Frémont had just returned. Going back there yet again could be hazardous, because California was Mexican territory.

The public greeted the report of Frémont's second frontier adventure with even more admiration than it had the first. Both Frémont and Jessie were becoming American heroes and seemingly enjoyed their newfound celebrity. According to Herr, "Eventually some would charge that for both him and Jessie, reputation—'this eternal vanity of how we must look'—had become more important than truth." To some it later seemed that the Frémonts were more interested in publicity than in documenting what happened. Of more immediate importance than fame for Jessie, though, was Frémont's impending departure.

Now a captain, Frémont left for the West on May 15, 1845. As before, Jessie was dejected at his departure. She followed his progress in newspaper accounts as he arrived in St. Louis to begin putting together the band of explorers that would travel with him. According to Herr:

> All summer long Jessie monitored the swell of enthusiasm for Frémont and the West. The newspapers continued to note his progress, and when the combined first and second reports were published in midsummer, the excitement reached a peak. . . . The initial government printing of twenty thousand copies quickly disappeared, and the next few years, at least twenty-two issues and editions—including five in Europe—were printed by private publishers. The reviews were as enthusiastic as the public response.

As had been expected, Frémont's trek into California came at the beginning of the conflict between Mexico and the United States. Mexican authorities asked him to leave in 1846, after he encouraged American settlers living in the Sacramento Valley to rebel and establish what was called the "Bear Flag" Republic, which they did that summer. The bear was chosen as their symbol because it stood for "ferocity, strength, and standing fast," according to Barbara R. Warner in her book *The Men of the California Bear Flag Revolt.*

A choice that Frémont later made was not as harmless as selecting a mascot for the California rebellion. When the Mexican War began, Frémont chose the wrong side in a dispute between two strong-willed American military officers: Commodore Robert Stockton of the U.S. Navy and Gen. Stephen W. Kearny of the U.S. Army, the same officer who had ordered the howitzer cannon for Frémont's earlier expedition. The disagreement arose over who should be in charge of the newly conquered California. Frémont sided with Stockton, and when Kearny won control of the territory, he charged Frémont with insubordination. He ordered that Frémont be arrested and stand trial in a court-martial.

When Jessie learned of her husband's fate she wanted to be with him. Against her father's protest at her traveling alone, she went to wait for Frémont in Kansas City. Even before they saw each other, Jessie knew there was more trouble. In the dedication of Fremont's *Memoirs*, she wrote: "Long before he arrived home, a cloud of miscomprehension concerning the facts had been manufactured. Certain newspapers teemed with inspired, bitter attacks against him, containing reports, similar to the untrue statements made later by General Kearny in giving his evidence." Then as now, leaks to the newspapers were made to influence public opinion. In this case, they were against Frémont. But Jessie would accept none of it; the bitterness she felt about the whole situation is apparent throughout the *Memoirs*. As in the past, and as she would in the future, she stood by her husband and was his principal defender.

Jessie and John traveled back to Washington together, meeting with her parents in Kentucky. The Missouri senator was ready to take on the Frémonts' enemies, including anyone who stood in their way or did not agree with their ideas concerning western expansion. Knowing that Jessie was familiar with the White House—she had been there many times as a child with

An early version of the future flag of the state of California, with the images of a bear and a star. Missourian William L. Todd contributed to the drawing of the flag. In a twist of historical irony, Todd was related to Mary Todd Lincoln, wife of President Abraham Lincoln; Frémont, who helped establish the state of California, and Lincoln clashed often during their careers. The original flag burnt in the aftermath of the 1906 San Francisco earthquake. (State Historical Society of Missouri, Columbia, courtesy of Bancroft Library, University of California, Berkeley)

her father—Frémont decided to use his wife to plead his cause. Never shy, Jessie was willing to take a bold step to help her husband: she and Kit Carson would go to the president and give him a personal letter from Frémont. Jessie had met Kit in 1842, when Frémont hired him to be his guide. Over the years they had become friends, and on this occasion she needed someone special to be by her side.

As was his custom, President James K. Polk allowed those with grievances or other issues they wanted to take up with the president to come into his office. When Jessie arrived with the other petitioners, Polk recognized her. She introduced Carson to him, and the president then took the letter that they presented. However, he did not reveal his thoughts, and Jessie and Kit left disappointed.

Throughout the court-martial, Jessie was at her husband's side. In January 1848 the court found Frémont guilty and ordered his dismissal from the army. Then President Polk entered into the case. He agreed with the court's decision, but according to the record he reversed the order. A document in the Frémont Family Papers at the University of California, Berkeley, discloses his reasoning that because "of previous meritorious and valuable service of Lieutenant-Colonel Frémont, and of the foregoing recommendations of the majority of the members of the court, the penalty of dismissal from the service is remitted. Lieutenant-Colonel Frémont will accordingly be released from arrest, will resume his sword and report for duty."

Polk's statement was not the end of the matter. Both Jessie and Frémont were furious with the court's original decision, and the president's subsequent action did nothing to change their minds. Neither of the Frémonts felt vindicated by the president's action. In their minds, he was offering a pardon for an act that Frémont had not committed, and to accept it would be an admission of guilt. Hence, Frémont replied to Polk: "I do not feel conscious of having done anything to merit the finding of the court and thus being the case I cannot, by accepting the clemency of the President admit the justice of the decree." The only honorable thing for Frémont to do, he and Jessie agreed, was for him to resign from the army. He did this on March 15, 1848, telling Polk, "I hereby send in my resignation of Lieut. Colonel of the Army of the United States."

After the court-martial, Jessie and Frémont worked together on an account of his trip to California. But the stress of recent events caught up with Jessie, who was pregnant with their second child, and while working on the project, she collapsed. Doctors ordered bed rest for her and Frémont finished work on the report. Once it was completed, he wanted a new beginning, and he suggested they settle in California. This would be a different journey. This time Jessie would join him.

CHAPTER 4

Jessie's Travels

*F*rémont's wish to start over in California was helped along by his father-in-law. While his influence was on the decline, the senator from Missouri still had important friends. Benton managed to arrange a privately funded trip to California for Frémont to search for a transcontinental railroad route through the Rocky Mountains. The trek did not start, though, until after the birth of the Fremonts' second child, Benton, on July 24, 1848.

The baby's godfather, Kit Carson, warned Jessie that her first-born son would not live long. He expressed his concern about Benton's fragile health when he attended the child's christening in Washington. Years later, in a letter to Carson, Jessie remembered his blunt words: "You were the first to warn me that my oldest boy could not live—I always think of you in connection with that poor suffering baby. Grief was new to me then and I could not bear to give him up. But that, and many another sorrow has come since you were with me at my Father's house—it makes what is left more valued." For now, "what is left" would come much later—the intended trip to California would come first.

Frémont planned to start his trip west from the St. Louis area, and Jessie wanted to see him off. So she, Frémont, their two children, and a nanny traveled to Missouri in the fall of 1848. It was in the frontier settlement of Westport Island, located on the Mississippi River near St. Louis in Lincoln County, that baby Benton died on October 6. After two days, and with Jessie's reluctant approval, his body was sent to St. Louis for burial. The grieving Frémont family continued their journey to the small town of Boone Creek in Franklin County, from where Frémont would begin his expedition. He and Jessie said their goodbyes, a hardship compounded by the loss of their son. Yet, as she wrote in her introduction to his *Memoirs,* their separation this time would be different: "[H]e must make the journey [by land] but I would go by sea and together we would make it [California] home." She returned to St. Louis and then Washington, and prepared for her trip to meet her husband in the spring. Jessie was about to see and do things that few people of any era ever did, especially women. As she reflected later, this trip "would be an ordeal that tried every feeling—an uprooting of every fiber." She was up to the challenge.

Jessie was eager to start a new life with her husband and daughter in California on the property Frémont had acquired. As she wrote in *Year,* "[T]he long expeditions which Mr. Frémont made took him from home five years of the first eight after we were married." Now it was Jessie's turn to go, to travel, and to explore new vistas. The plan was for her father to go with her to the American West, the land of newly discovered gold— a place he had dreamed of for so long. However, as the time for the trip arrived, Benton, for reasons that are not known, did not join Jessie. As she related in *Year,* her father "found himself unable to go from home." She gave no further explanation.

There were two ways to get to California in 1849. One choice was to traverse the continent overland—an almost impossible task with no established transportation in place. Companies and individuals such as Kit Carson would escort groups to California for a price, about $100. The fee usually included mules for a wagon, three months of provisions, and the invaluable expertise needed to guide travelers across America's frontier. Such companies kept the wagons in their troupe to a small number, for ease of travel and safety.

The second alternative was the one Jessie selected: to sail down the East Coast of the United States to Panama, cross the

CIVILIAN,

170 tons, newly coppered, and four years old, Commanded by

Capt. Thomas Dodge,

of Chatham, will sail for California Oct. 20th. She is owned by the " COCHITUATE COMPANY for California," now nearly full. She is fitted up with Superior Accommodations, is a fast sailing vessel, and offers advantages equal to if not superior to any vessel that has yet been put up.

Please call for information at No. 69 Commercial Street.

Boston, Sept. 27th. 1849.   **E. W. JACKSON, Agent.**

Rand & Co's Job Press, 3 Cornhill.

While it does not picture the *Crescent City,* the boat that took Jessie and Lily to Panama, this advertisement is typical of those that ship companies used to lure passengers to the California gold fields via Panama. *(Attention, Pioneers!* James S. Copley Library) isthmus by boat, canoe, and mule, and then catch a steamer that took travelers up the West Coast to California and its newly discovered gold mines. This option was much more expensive. Steamship prices for sailing from New York to the port of Chagres, on Panama's east coast, ranged from $100 to $150. Then there were other costs: to cross the isthmus the usual fee was $35, and the voyage from Panama to California brought another charge ranging from $150 to $300. Most settlers or "forty-niners" could not afford this route to the West. In addition to the numerous expenses, it was also a daunting and arduous journey.

While Benton could not make the voyage with his daughter, he did travel to New York in March 1849 to see her and six-year-old Lily off, but this did not ease Jessie's trepidation about the trip. She explained her feelings in *Year*:

> My father's going with me would have made it a delightful voyage for both of us; without him, it was, in all its dreary bleakness, my first separation from home. . . . I had never been obliged to think for or take care of myself, and now I was to be launched literally on an unknown sea, travel towards an unknown country, everything absolutely new and strange about me, and undefined for the future and without even a servant that knew me.

Her fears were certainly understandable. To join her husband, she would have to travel by steamship, boat, and mule—a grueling undertaking. To allay her concerns, her father engaged a servant to travel with her, since no one from the Benton household staff was available. Unfortunately, the person he hired did not work out, so Jessie traveled alone with her young daughter. Her brother-in-law, Richard Taylor Jacob, her sister Sarah's husband, was on the same ship. He was making the voyage for his health, but he was so seasick that he was unable to offer company or assistance. With Jessie and her daughter aboard, along with hundreds of gold-seeking forty-niners, the *Crescent City* left a cold New York on March 15, 1849, and sailed off to the warmer climes of Panama. The ultimate destination for all its passengers was California and the bright future they hoped it would bring to them.

Jessie and Lily reached the Panamanian isthmus on March 24 after a nine-day sail from New York; then the truly tough part of their journey began: crossing Panama. If Jessie could have had it her way, she would not have made the trek at all. She described her feelings in *Year*: "When we reached Chagres, if it had not been for pure shame and unwillingness that my father should think badly of me, I would have returned to New York on the steamer." The next boat Jessie took did not make traveling any easier; Lily described it in *Recollections of Elizabeth Benton Frémont* as a "little tender . . . as small as a craft could well be and yet hold an engine." Despite the fact that their "large double cabin" was the best compartment, the trip was certainly difficult.

Once the little ship could no longer navigate the inlets in Panama, the passengers transferred to dugout canoes to continue their travel—all the passengers except Jessie and Lily, that is. "We were spared the terrors of the dugout canoes. . . . [W]e were permitted to travel in [a] whale boat, manned by a responsible crew," Lily wrote. The owner of the steamship company knew who Jessie was and permitted her the luxury, such as it was, to ride in better style. The boat was in reality just a bit larger than a canoe, but it did have palm leaves that offered a cover from the brutally hot sun.

Progress was slow. Navigating the waterways was done by placing poles in the water and then pushing on them to propel the boat against the river currents. Only a short distance each day could be made this way. At night, the vessels pulled to shore. Lily described the scene in her book: "Most of the travelers of those days were compelled to take their chances of sleeping on the ground or in the huts of the Indians, and all too often con-tracted fevers from the night air and the tropical mists." However, because the steamship company was looking after the Frémonts, their situation was better. Jessie wrote in *Year* that they had a tent, "with its canvas floor and walls, lit up by the great fire outside. . . . [O]ur clean linen cots were very welcome

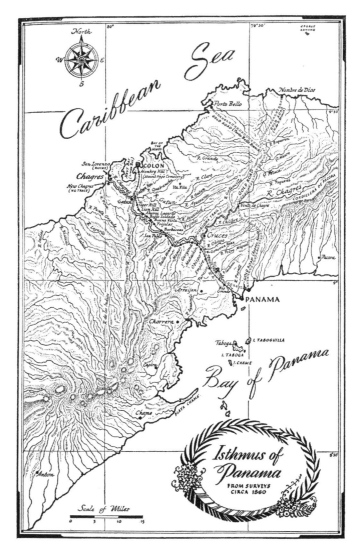

Map showing the topography of the land route across the Panamanian isthmus that Jessie and Lily traveled in 1849. With no railroad or canal yet built to make traveling easier, the trail from the mouth of the Chagres River to Panama City took a heavy toll on those who made the passage. (*The Chagres: River of Westward Passage*, James S. Copley Library)

after the fatigue of the day, with all of its excitement and new ideas."

Soon the canoes and whaleboat were abandoned for mules, because that was the only way to get over the mountains and reach Panama City, where, if you were lucky, you could catch a steamer up the coast to California. In *Year*, Jessie gave a vivid account of the twenty-one mile trek over the mountains:

> There was only a mule track—rather a trough than track in most places, and mule staircases with occasional steps of at least four feet, and only wide enough for a single animal . . . straight up the sides of the steepest heights to the summit, then straight down then again to the base. No bridges across the rapid streams. These had to be forded by the mules, or, when narrow, the mule would gather his legs under him and leap it. If one could sit him, so much the better; if not, one fell into the water; and in this way many emigrants got broken bones, and many more bruises and thorough wettings.

Jessie did not remark on her own fate regarding broken bones, bruises, or a fall into the water!

After two days of this type of travel, Jessie, her daughter, and the others in their band of hearty souls reached Panama City in April 1849. Now came the task of finding lodging while waiting for transportation north to California. Some were fortunate enough to find accommodations in hastily constructed hotels built for those heading to the California gold fields, thus avoiding having to sleep on the docks or elsewhere. Jessie and Lily fared better. Jessie wrote: "An elderly lady, a widow, made me come to her house and remain with her during my whole stay; there, with her daughters and her nice old servants, I had none of the forlornness which belongs to being in a hotel, and quickly slipped into a routine very much like my ordinary life, only with very different scenery and actors." Being the wife of a noted explorer paid dividends for Jessie.

Finding transportation to California was not so easy. Ships

that came from Panama and docked in San Francisco often lost not only their passengers to the gold fields but their crews as well, making travel between California and Panama very irregular at best. Thousands of forty-niners milled around the Panamanian waterfront awaiting overdue steamers. Jessie, however, bided her time in the safety and security of a pleasant Spanish home, writing and answering correspondence, reading, and enjoying the vistas of Panama. This tranquility soon ended.

First came news of Frémont's failure to find a path through the Rocky Mountains. During the trek, eleven men died from cold and starvation. Frémont blamed William Sherley Williams, the famed Missouri guide known as Old Bill Williams. Frémont wrote to Jessie, "The error of our journey was committed in engaging this man." Others blamed the expedition leader for insisting on taking the group through the mountains in the dead of winter and failing to follow Williams's advice about the best route.

Second, and more importantly, Jessie became very ill. Lung disorders—particularly tuberculosis, or consumption, as it was commonly known—were prevalent in the Benton family. Now it was Jessie who was afflicted with this horrible illness. Both Spanish and American doctors were summoned to treat her congested lungs and bloody cough. According to Jessie, "These two, with their contradictory ideas and their inability to understand each other fully, only added to the confusion of my mind, and became part of my delirium." Leeches were ordered but none were found. Luckily the cough and fever subsided and the crisis passed. While Jessie remained weak, she was soon well enough to board a ship for California.

She waited seven long weeks in Panama for a vessel to arrive to take her and Lily to meet Frémont; on May 6, not one, but two steamers arrived—one from New York, the other from California. Aboard the California ship was a traveler whom Jessie knew. He urged her to return east with him, saying he had heard that Frémont was leaving California and returning home. Conflicted, Jessie decided that she would continue on despite the rumor that her husband had left the West, believing that he would keep his promise to meet her in California. So, on May 18, 1849, she and Lily boarded the *Panama*, which was packed with travelers hoping to find gold in California.

Their cabin was stuffy and stifling, and Jessie's cough returned. To help her, she wrote, the crew "made me a room on the quarter-deck with the big flag doubled and thrown over the boom. Everybody contributed something to make me feel comfortable: one a folding iron cam bedstead—some, guava jelly—some tea." This "flag tent" became her cabin and the fresh air helped to ease her cough, with "the pure air of the ocean coming into my lungs night and day and healing them."

Jessie's trip up the coast was pleasant and uneventful. As the ship neared San Diego, she grew fearful that she would not find her husband: Was he well? Had he gone east? Would he meet her in San Francisco as they had planned? When the ship docked in San Diego, she went to her muggy cabin to wait for news. Soon, crewmembers came to her door with the happy report that Frémont was on his way to San Francisco to meet her and Lily. In later years her trips to California would be much easier because during the 1850s, as a result of the gold rush, Panama built a trans-isthmus railroad. On future journeys Jessie traveled by train, lunch included, with only a brief stay in Panama City before taking a ship up the west coast to California. What a different journey!

This first trip, though, changed Jessie: she had met many hardships and survived. A world that she had heard about from her father and her husband opened to her. She had left the constraints of eastern society behind. She allowed herself to accept the West's excitement and frankness—traits that Benton and Frémont had long ago recognized and admired. Jessie was now ready to start anew and begin a fresh life in California. She was one of many people, from many places, who for generations have sought a new beginning in the American West. In Jessie's case, her adventures would continue.

CHAPTER 5

California

*A*fter three months of travel, Jessie and Lily arrived in San Francisco filled with various emotions: happy finally to be in California; excited to be reunited with John, husband and father; and perhaps, too, a bit dismayed at what they saw. In June of 1849, San Francisco was a town of tents ringing the bottom of the city's foothills, with only a few actual houses built. The famed bay had numerous deserted ships anchored in it, abandoned by their owners and crew members, who had left them to find their fortunes in the gold fields. Getting ashore was problematic for travelers: ship captains had no control over their crews, who, after rowing passengers ashore, often left for the gold mines instead of returning to the boat to transport additional passengers into the city.

Jessie was hopeful that she would see John in San Francisco, after learning in San Diego that he had not returned east. However, as rowboats from shore paddled out to meet the steamer, she soon realized that he was not in any of them. She had a choice to make: she could wait on board the steamer until John traveled up the California coast, or she could accept an offer from "[William] Howard, a wealthy merchant, who had brought out his boat to go ashore." As she wrote in *Year*, she was tired of sea travel "and land was best for me," so she accepted Howard's offer. A prominent resident of the city, he found lodging for Jessie and Lily in one of San Francisco's better houses.

The home turned out to be the residence of a deceased Russian consul, with "luxuries of every kind . . . a beautiful gar-

San Francisco Bay in 1849. This is the sight that greeted Jessie when she arrived. Note the ships in the harbor, many abandoned by their crews because they left for the gold fields, leaving passengers to fend for themselves in getting ashore. (State Historical Society of Missouri, Columbia)

den . . . fine carpets and fine furniture and a fine Broadwood piano. . . . [T]he one room with a fireplace had been prepared for my sleeping room, and had French furniture and no end of mirrors." Jessie received such favors because she was the daughter of a distinguished senator and the wife of a famous explorer. Jessie and Frémont often accepted the largesse extended to well-known people according to the custom of the day. She was indeed fortunate, because the majority of dwellings in the city were "canvas and blanket tents." However, it was in very comfortable lodgings that she and Lily waited for Frémont.

Until her husband came, Jessie busied herself with San Francisco society, such as it was. The city was bustling: lively and frenetic with miners coming and going, and raucous with new arrivals. Vendors sold their merchandise in tents because "there was no lumber there for building, and there were not even trees to be cut down nor would any man have diverted his attention from the mines" to build any structures. Once the news of Jessie's arrival spread, she met with many people who took time out of their busy pursuits to welcome her to California.

As Jessie waited, the dank climate of San Francisco began to take its toll on her and she became ill again with the lung problems that had plagued her in Panama. Ten days after Jessie arrived, Frémont finally made it to San Francisco, and he took charge of the situation. Jessie recalled that they traveled "by steamer to Monterey, where there was a very different climate." The Frémont family finally arrived at their new home on June 20, 1849.

Jessie had a difficult time adjusting to frontier life. Monterey was not San Francisco—"there was none of the stir and life here which made San Francisco so remarkable"—nor was it Virginia, Washington, or St. Louis. She confronted a different lifestyle, one that in no way resembled that of her previous upper-class existence. She coped. In *Year*, she described her new life:

> It was barely a year since the gold had been discovered, but in that time every eatable thing had been eaten off the face of the country, and nothing raised. I suppose there was not a fowl left in the northern part of the state, consequently not an egg. . . . There were no cows, consequently no milk. Housekeeping, deprived of milk, eggs, vegetables, and fresh meat, becomes a puzzle; canned meat, macaroni, rice, and ham become unendurable from repetition. . . . [W]hile wood was abundant around here, there was no one to cut it.

The small community of Monterey welcomed the Frémonts, but finding housing was a problem. They had to rent part of a hacienda, though it was not just any Spanish villa. It was "the largest and best building in town . . . the [former Mexican] Governor's residence; it occupied double the usual space, and was really a good building, with very thick walls, and a charming

Bear Valley, California, in 1859. It was here that Jessie turned the family's wooden cottage into a home. (Huntington Library, San Marino, California)

great garden, surrounded by a hedge of roses." People provided Jessie and her family with food, wood for the fireplace, and friendship. Once again, because of who they were, the Frémonts were able to take advantage of their reputations to satisfy their immediate needs.

They were treated as celebrities, even by those long-time residents of California, the Indians and Mexicans, who considered the Frémont name a symbol of "invasion and defeat," as Jessie wrote in *Year*. In 1848, after two years of war—a bitter conflict in which Frémont played a major role—the United States had conquered Mexico and forced it to surrender California. Yet, after the Frémont family spent some time in Monterey, Jessie found the residents there "among the kindest people I knew," she recalled. Members of the tiny California settlement were always coming to their aid. She wrote: "The only cow in town belonged to one of these [Mexicans], and she sent daily a portion of the milk, because I too had a little child."

Despite the generosity of those around them, there were still tribulations for Jessie to confront, especially since she had never managed a household by herself. There was food to cook, baking to be done, clothes to make and mend, laundry to do, and a child to watch. Jessie needed assistance, but domestic help was scarce. She was rescued from the drudgery of household chores when a woman from Sydney, Australia, came to Monterey look-ing for work. She and Jessie found each other and soon Jessie's home was running smoothly. Her health improved, her strength was restored, and she was ready to travel around her newly adopted home in her favorite form of transportation—her spe-cial carriage.

Once the Frémonts decided to move to California, they arranged for their possessions to be transported to them. The Frémont Papers at the Bancroft Library disclose that a supply vessel named the U.S.S. *Fredonia* traveled around the Horn with "a sawmill [for Frémont's business ventures] and many useful domestic things for a new country." One of the items shipped was a six-seated carriage for Jessie. Built in New Jersey, it was designed with comfort in mind. But it required horses accus-tomed to harness, and California horses were not used to such tackle. Frémont was never able to find the right animals and had to settle for a pair of mules that would accommodate the car-riage. This coach became Jessie's main source of transportation as she journeyed about middle California—San Jose, San Fran-cisco, and of course Monterey. In her book *Recollections*, Lily described the trips this way:

> We lived a nomadic life at first, driving back and forth between San José, Monterey and San Francisco, very rarely sleeping even for one night under a roof. My mother had the cushions drawn together in the surrey so as to form a mattress, while I slept in the boot. . . . Often during the day time, we would stop for awhile at one or another of the numerous Spanish ranches, where we were always made welcome by both men and women.

Jessie thoroughly enjoyed these wanderings through California. In *Year* she reflected: "I was charmed with every detail of my camping life. The carriage, all its curtains rolled up . . . [and] after us, at a little distance, was our baggage train—a string of mules packed with our cooking apparatus . . . and such clothes that we could pack." At night the men, including Frémont, slept in the open, either on blankets or on grass hammocks tied between trees. To call these journeys camping trips is not quite accurate by today's standards, however, because Jessie was pampered. She traveled in style: "My early cup of tea was brought to the carriage to me at dawn. We always camped at the side of a brook, and a dressing-tent was quickly made for me with a pair of blankets; I had a tin basin, plenty of towels, plenty of French soap and Cologne water." The settlers the Frémonts met along the way were always eager to hear of news from the "states," and Jessie gladly shared whatever information she had from home. This was true even if the request was in Spanish, because she was fluent in that language, having learned it and other foreign languages as a young girl.

Most of these camping ventures were undertaken during the drier weather, which made travel easier and helped restore Jessie to robust health. However, as the time approached for what passes for the rainy season in California, the Frémonts headed home to Monterey. Besides, there was business to oversee.

The Frémonts were forty-niners, too, though not in the usual sense. John did not go to the gold fields with a pick, pan, or shovel. In 1847, before leaving California to face his court-martial, Frémont gave a friend, Thomas O. Larkin, the first and last American consul to Mexico's California territory, $3,000 to acquire property near the city of San Francisco. Instead Larkin purchased over 44,000 acres of mineral and agricultural lands in Mariposa County, south and east of the city. Frémont had mines, lumber assets, and as many water rights as he could acquire. He had paid laborers, along with machines, to do the actual searching for gold and whatever other minerals might be found. In addition to the valuable land, ultimately there was a house. The

An artist's rendition of men panning for gold during the California gold rush. This is the conventional view of the "forty-niner" and his quest for instant fortune. (State Historical Society of Missouri, Columbia)

entire holdings, including the ranch, were subsequently valued at $10 million. The family did not live on the vast property all of the time when they moved to California; in the summer the heat could be unbearable and often they made trips to other parts of the state to escape the high temperatures.

While on a family camping trip in 1849, Frémont received word that one of his mines had "panned out." At a stop in San Jose, he took delivery of his first "convoy of gold." Because there were no banks or other financial institutions, "the buckskin bags, containing about a hundred pounds of gold, were put for safety under the straw mattress." This gold and other amounts Frémont received ended up in Monterey, "and it accumulated in trunks in our rooms there," Jessie wrote. It seemed that the Frémonts would no longer have to depend on the generosity of

In contrast to the traditional way of searching for gold with a pick, shovel, and pan, entrepreneurs like Frémont used hydraulic and other mechanical devices to hunt for the precious ore. *(Up and Down California in 1860–1864,* James S. Copley Library)

friends. Jessie rejoiced: "[W]e were young and full of health, and in all the exhilaration of sudden wealth which could enable us to realize our greatest wishes." As the years went on, the Frémont fortune would disappear as the result of John's poor financial dealings, especially investments in railroad plans that did not work out. For now, though, life was good for Jessie and John. And soon, when John entered politics, it seemed that all their dreams might come true.

There was a need to quickly establish a government for California—lawlessness prevailed due to the rapid influx of people brought by the gold rush. The process of bringing about order to what would become the "golden state" began in Monterey in 1849. Prominent California settlers held meetings to establish a state legislature that eventually convened in San Jose. One of the responsibilities of the new government was to select men to represent California in the U.S. Senate. John Charles Frémont was chosen to be one of the state's first U.S. senators. He was following in the footsteps of his father-in-law, who was one of the first U.S. senators from Missouri. Jessie could not have been happier.

By tradition, senators from each state serve staggered six-year terms so that both do not stand for election at the same time. California was a new state, with two new senate seats to fill. Literally by drawing straws, Frémont won the short term—from September 1850 to March 1851—with the longer six-year term going to William Gwin. When his term was up, Frémont wanted a full term, but new political factions in the state thwarted his reelection. However, for now, not even his drawing the short term could dampen Jessie's joy. Nothing mattered but the fact that the Frémonts were going home. Jessie explained: "I had been gone but a year and a day when I was again back in my father's house."

Jessie enjoyed being reunited with her family and friends and sharing in the activities of the Washington scene. However, the reunion was short and the joy fleeting: she and John were back in California by early 1851 once his Senate term ended. On April 19 another son, John Charles Frémont, was born. After Charley's birth, Jessie and John decided to go to Europe for an extended vacation. Everywhere they went, people greeted them with acclaim, and their warm welcome added to the joy of the birth of another daughter, Anne Beverly Frémont, in Paris on February 1, 1853. The yearlong vacation and the happiness of a new child ended in 1853 when they returned to the United States, where Anne died on July 11.

Once back in America, Frémont rented a house in Washington next to the Benton home and planned for one more expedition west. With his family provided for, he headed to St. Louis in September 1853 to make preparations for a winter expedition. Leaving in November, he would cross the continent in hopes once again of learning what effect harsh wintry weather would have on possible railroad routes across the country. Whenever it was possible, Jessie made a habit of bidding farewell to her husband when he left on one his many excursions west. Her trip in the autumn of 1853 was notable, not because it was once again difficult to say goodbye, but because getting back home was complicated.

She journeyed to Independence, Missouri, to see Frémont off, and was going back to St. Louis when the water level of the Missouri River became too low for boats to navigate. Jessie left her ship at Washington, Missouri. She felt no alarm. In her book *The Story of the Guard*, Jessie wrote: "I had so often gone to the frontier with Mr. Frémont, when he was starting on his overland journeys, or to meet him on his return, that my associations with the State were of the hospitality and kind sympathy so often and so warmly given to me by its people."

Jessie needed a place to stay overnight. She found her way to the "'best room' of a large house, whose mistress and daughter came forward and made me quietly welcome as though they knew me." At first she kept her identity to herself, but she finally told her German hosts who she was and they treated her like royalty, explaining that they greatly admired her father.

Despite the generosity shown her, Jessie was on her way at daybreak. In *Guard* she described her departure: "Very early the next morning I started to make the intervening twenty-seven miles [to St. Louis], in the best conveyance the sudden demand could afford—a country-cart without springs, and a plough-horse. And so, in the gray dawn, I left these kind people, loaded with presents from their best vintages for my father, followed by their kindest good wishes for myself." No wonder that Jessie could say "anywhere in Missouri I felt at home."

Frémont returned home in May 1854 after a difficult western trek. While the homecoming was joyous, the family soon faced many changes. The first was the death of Jessie's mother, Elizabeth Benton, on September 10, 1854. Six months later, on March 26, 1855, a "funeral discourse" was delivered in her honor in the Second Presbyterian Church in St. Louis. The service was presided over by the Reverend Nathan Lewis Rice, who said of Mrs. Benton:

> She was endowed with an intellect of extraordinary vigor, which was highly cultivated. She possessed a remarkable firmness of purpose and great moral courage, which combined with an amiable and affectionate disposition, secured for her both the respect and the love of those who knew her. She was one of the pioneers amongst the Presbyterians of St. Louis—having come to the city at a time when there were not more than one or two Presbyterian families, and when the little band worshipped in a school house. The position of public life occupied by her husband, threw Mrs. B., during the whole of her married life into the gayest and most worldly circles; but she was never fascinated by them. . . . Her light shone with a steady brightness here, in public and in private, in the capacities of wife, mother, friend.

The death of Jessie's mother affected the entire family. In *Recollections*, Lily wrote: "After the death of my grandmother, who had been an invalid for years, my grandfather spent more time in St. Louis than had been his custom during her life, and, after a summer spent at Siasconset, Nantucket Island, we settled down in New York instead of returning to Washington."

The problems and issues of the coming years would not only shape the Frémonts' future but would also change the course of national events. They could be summed up into what Lily referred to as "the slavery question." Long bubbling beneath the surface of America's social fabric, the conflict over slavery was about to erupt and tear the country apart. The Frémonts, like most Americans, could not escape the coming division, nor could they escape the Civil War. In fact, they would be caught up in the upheaval leading to war, entangled in events during the war, and embroiled in controversy with the president of the United States, Abraham Lincoln. Jessie would be at the very center of all this chaos.

CHAPTER 6

"Fair Jessie"

*M*ost likely Jessie thought she had left the world of active politics behind when her husband's senate term ended. If so, she was wrong. In 1856, John Charles Frémont would be a candidate for the office of president of the United States. The attempt to attain America's highest office required tough campaigning—something Jessie did not shirk. However, it also created a situation she abhorred: a rift with her father.

By 1856, America was moving toward Civil War and the Frémonts would each play an important role in the coming hostilities. The central issue in that conflict was slavery—a problem that began in 1619 when the first slave ship, a Dutch vessel, docked in Jamestown, Virginia, with a cargo of Africans who were sold to the highest bidder. Historically, it is not known whether this first shipment of Africans became slaves or indentured servants—people who sold their services in return for passage to the new world. What is known is that it was the first time Africans were sold into servitude in the colonies. By the 1640s regulations were imposed on Africans entering the colony of Virginia, and permanent restrictions known as slave codes were in place by the 1660s. So began the tortuous history of black slavery in the United States. As Americans moved westward across the continent, they took all their belongings with them—including those enslaved by the "peculiar institution."

The settlement movement to the South presented no major political problem relating to slavery, despite the fact that abolitionists were present in the colonies, and subsequently in the states, almost from the time slavery was established in America. By the mid-1830s the movement gained strong national attention and political concerns began when settlers started moving into the midwestern section of America. In places such as Missouri, Kansas, and Nebraska, the debate over "free soil" versus slave territory became heated and at times violent. While there was not a widespread economic base or need for slavery in these regions as there was in the Deep South, such as the Mississippi delta area with its plantation-based society, the practice did exist in America's heartland. Slavery became a political issue in any region that slaveholders moved to because they wanted to take all of their "property" with them—especially their "chattel," the legal term for slaves.

To use the term *slavery* only in relation to agricultural pursuits would be misleading. Slavery found its way into cities, into businesses, into a nascent industrialized country. In *Agriculture and Slavery in Missouri's Little Dixie*, R. Douglas Hurt covers this topic well. Missourians utilized their slaves in the traditional agricultural way, to be sure, working them on farms that cultivated a variety of crops, including tobacco and hemp. However, because there were not enough people to meet the demand for farm workers, because there was a need for labor in homes and towns, and because the supply of white labor was almost nonexistent, slaves were also hired out. Hurt explains: "[F]armers often did not own slaves, but they supported the institution and hired slaves from masters who had an excess labor supply." He adds: "Masters . . . customarily advertised in the local newspapers, noting that their servants were good farm and domestic workers. These masters could substantially supplement their annual incomes in this manner." This custom often led owners to the realization that it was more profitable to find employment for their slaves than to maintain their property themselves. Thus, slavery became a business unto itself.

To regulate this arrangement of hiring out, a contract system was devised. Hurt writes:

These contracts detailed the obligations of the employer regarding the provision of summer and winter clothing and the payment of all taxes and doctor's bills for the slave. Restrictions often included prohibiting the employer from taking the bondsman out of the county or from hiring him or her to a third party. If the slave was not returned to his master on the date due, the hiring party became obligated to pay "legal interest" on the total fee until the slave was returned.

The "liberal wages" that were paid of course went to the owner and not the slaves. Slaves who were hired for agricultural work or factory production "could be easily exploited by employers who drove them beyond reasonable expectations."

No matter what the type of slavery, no matter how or where slaves were used, the Missouri Territory became involved in an emotional debate when it petitioned for statehood in 1818. At the time, there were twenty-two states: eleven free and eleven slave. Since Missouri permitted slavery, the belief was that it would come into the Union as a slave state, thus upsetting the balance of political power in the U.S. Senate, where each state had two senators and slavery advocates held sway. The House of Representatives, based on population, gave the more densely inhabited free states the edge. A bitter struggle thus began, with each side wanting to gain something so it could claim victory.

The resolve of the antislavery side came to the forefront when New York congressman James Tallmadge offered a proposal to amend the bill that would allow Missouri to enter the Union. His idea was to prohibit Missouri from bringing in any more slaves after admission; in addition, any slaves born after statehood would become free at the age of twenty-five. Such a plan, over time, would eliminate slavery from Missouri. The House supported the Tallmadge Amendment, the Senate did not, and Congress adjourned without settling the question of Missouri's admission. The territory would have to wait until the following year, when a compromise ultimately materialized.

The next session of Congress, in 1819, brought a glimmer of

hope for Missouri. The territory of Maine asked for admission as a free state, and that, along with Missouri's admission as a slave state, would keep the national political balance of power intact, at least in the Senate. This situation led to the Missouri Compromise. Maine became part of the United States on March 15, 1820, but Missouri had to wait yet another year. The delay was due to the fact that Missouri needed to write a state constitution. Even this task caused a snafu. Congress would never approve a document that did not allow free blacks or mulattoes to enter a state, which is precisely what Missourians wanted in their state constitution. It was necessary to work out a second compromise. The new document provided for the legalization of slavery in the state and stipulated that Missouri would not deny American black citizens their constitutional rights. This last provision was something of a contradiction, since American blacks had no constitutional rights until after the Civil War. Finally, though, Missouri entered the Union on August 10, 1821. It was the twenty-fourth state.

Missouri's admission to the Union did not end the discussion about slavery and all of its ramifications; debate continued up to and through the Civil War. Many Americans such as Sen. Thomas Hart Benton believed that nothing—and certainly not slavery—should deter the country from its manifest destiny to spread from the Atlantic to the Pacific Ocean. Benton, even at the risk of losing political support, opposed the extension of slavery to any new western territory. His daughter Jessie embraced this belief as well. Politicians desperately tried, in the decades after the slave codes appeared first in the territories and then in the states, to heal the rift with various types of legislation and compromise, but in the end nothing worked. It was as if the slavery issue was a wound on the conscience of America that would not heal and that would imperil the country's future.

According to Hurt, many Missourians, not just politicians, were caught up in the debate over whether slavery should be allowed to spread throughout America and its territories:

By the late 1840s, abolitionism had divided Missourians, especially those in central Missouri. Most residents . . . advocated the extension of slavery into the territories, and many favored congressional silence or nonintervention on the issue. They believed that if slaveholders chose to take their bondsmen into the territories, they should be allowed to do so. Upon the formation of new states [and] drafting of new constitutions, the doctrine of popular sovereignty could determine the status of slavery. This position did not mean that the residents of [Missouri] were ready to abandon the institution. In fact, from the beginning of the abolitionist movement . . . Missourians had wanted both slavery and Union.

In the years immediately before the Civil War, and surely by 1856, the country was on the verge of being torn asunder over the question of whether slavery should be a part of the Union. Many people in and out of government, many influential citizens, and many ordinary people thought the only hope to save the Union was to form a new political party, one that directly confronted the issue. The person they chose to lead this party to a hoped-for victory in the next presidential election was John Charles Frémont.

Frémont was a good fit for this new political party—the Republican Party. He had excellent credentials: he was certainly well-known all across the country because of his western expeditions, thanks in large part to Jessie's skillful narrations of his journeys. It was recognized that he opposed slavery and its spread into the western territories. In the debate over whether California would come into the Union as a slave state or free state, Frémont sided with the "free soilers." He knew that if he used slaves at his mines it would bring in more profit, but instead he paid free men to work for him. He was chided by his peers for this decision, but he held steadfast, "determined to sink or swim in the sea of fortune with free labor," as Lily put it in her *Recollections*. Jessie stood by his side in this decision. Lily described her parents' point of view:

My mother worked as hard as did my father for the admission of the free state [California], . . . cheerfully doing her own work rather than take any steps that might influence the adoption of slavery into our splendid territory. . . . My mother by birth and tradition was opposed to slavery. Her mother, a Virginian, . . . had after the death of her father, . . . immediately freed all the slaves he had left her, starting some of them in trades, sending others to Canada or Liberia as they preferred, and always looking out for those who remained in the United States.

My father believed in those days that California was the paradise of free labor, an opinion that he never changed to the end of his days.

These were the views that Jessie and John brought to the presidential campaign of 1856.

The Republican Party, which came to be known as the Grand Old Party after the Civil War, developed because many people, in and out of the political system, opposed extending slavery into the territories. After its founding in Jackson, Michigan, in 1854, it gained numerous seats in the U.S. House of Representatives, but never enough to outvote or outmaneuver the Democrats, who were the majority party and predominantly proslavery. However, by 1856, the Republicans felt confident enough to run a candidate for president, and that candidate was Frémont.

Jessie and her family were living in Nantucket, Massachusetts, when the offer came—but it was not the nascent GOP that approached Frémont first. Representatives of the Democratic Party, long the party of the Bentons, approached Frémont with a proposal they hoped would entice him to be *their* presidential candidate. Lily described this development in her book: "On account of his well known aversion to slavery, it was suggested that the party platform would permit alternate states to come into the Union as slave and free, but my father would sign no plank that did not make for absolute freedom." He refused the Democrats' offer.

Political cartoon showing why a vote for Frémont—and, by implication, Jessie—is better than a vote for his rival, James Buchanan. The message is to look forward to the future with the new Republican Party, rather than backward to the past with the old Democratic Party. (Huntington Library)

After the Democratic attempt failed, the Republicans made their move. They approached Frémont after he and his family returned to New York City from their summer stay in Nantucket. Again, Lily explained the events: "On the 27th of June [1856], the Republican party, in its first national convention at Philadelphia, nominated my father to head the ticket." Both Jessie and her husband felt comfortable with the turn of events, except for the family rift that it would cause.

Jessie saw clearly what this first nationwide campaign by the Republican Party would mean for her family. She knew the anguish her husband's decision would cause among the Benton clan—the daughter and son-in-law of a famed Democrat and former U.S. senator turning their backs on a long family tradition and heritage. She understood what she was doing and recognized that she was saying good-bye to her past, yet she faced the campaign with energy.

While Jessie was determined to help her husband win the White House, she was dismayed that her father could not be persuaded by family, friends, or sympathetic politicians to support him. Benton was adamantly opposed to the ideas of the Republican Party, despite the fact that he did not support slavery or its extension into the opening West. He believed that a new political organization solely tied to that idea would rip the country apart. He hoped that his party, the Democratic Party, would somehow find a way to deal with the issue of slavery. He was disappointed that his beloved daughter supported the opposition, and even more disappointed that the opposition was led by her husband. Reconciliation between father and daughter would not come until long after the campaign was over, especially since Benton endorsed Frémont's Democratic rival, James Buchanan.

Not only did Jessie support her husband, she also became a part of the campaign of 1856. The most often-heard rally cry was "Frémont and Jessie." Another slogan was "Free Speech, Free Press, Free Soil, Free Men, Frémont and Victory." It was behind the scenes, however, that Jessie had her most important job. Lily explained what her mother did:

> [The] campaign was full of personalities, and my father's nature was such that he could not have withstood its bitterness. He was used to life in the open and wanted a square fight, not one filled with petty innuendoes and unfounded recrimination. So at the outset, it was agreed that he should not read his mail during the campaign, nor read the newspapers until they had been blue-penciled by my mother.

Frémont must have been very naive to think that his run for the presidency would not be raucous, and some of the "recriminations" were indeed harsh. From the beginning of the

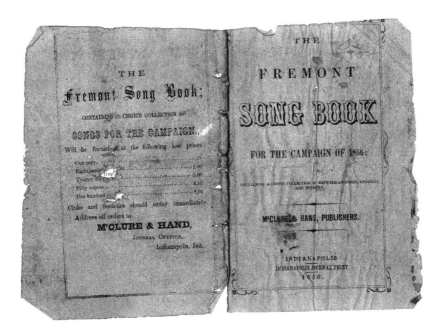

In an era before radio and television, political songs were the way to tell the public about candidates. *The Fremont Song Book,* compiled for the 1856 campaign, put words to popular tunes of the day such as "Camptown Races" and "Oh! Susanna." A typical verse went: "Old Bullion had a daughter fair, Jessie was her name, / The Rocky Mountain Traveler a courting her he came, / He wooed her and he won her, and will make her, by the fates, / The Lady of the President of these United States." (Frémont Letters and Papers, James S. Copley Library)

American republic, presidential elections have been filled with insinuations and smears, and the campaign of 1856 was no different—it was nasty. Seasoned as she was, because she was raised in a political household, Jessie was prepared for the rough-and-tumble of a political campaign. For example, there were allegations that Frémont was a Catholic, which he was not, but it was something Protestant America would not tolerate (the United States did not have a Catholic president until John F. Kennedy won in 1960); that he was illegitimate, which he technically was; and that he was a poor manager of his business holdings, which he was. As if all of this was not enough, there was also a sex scandal.

There were allegations that Frémont had been unfaithful to his wife—standard political fodder for a presidential campaign of any time period. Newspaper stories suggested that when Frémont was in Los Angeles, "he kept 'a public harem' where he lured local 'sisters, mothers, and daughters.'" Naturally, these allegations hurt Jessie the most, even when Frémont denied them.

None of these accusations deterred her, though, nor was she slowed down by the fact that she had a new baby to care for. She was now thirty, and her fifth and last child, Frank Preston Frémont, was born on May 17, 1855. Jessie in fact seemed to enjoy her new role. Everywhere she went, she was greeted with excitement and enthusiasm as the daughter of one of America's well-known political leaders and the wife of a famed American explorer, now a presidential candidate. It is important to remember that during the nineteenth century women were just beginning to take part in society after decades of required demureness. While they had begun to be involved in antislavery and women's rights crusades, they still were not part of any major political campaigning. Jessie was breaking many barriers, entering into new arenas for a woman. Posters featuring her likeness were everywhere and songs featuring her in their lyrics were written and sung. One musical number had these words: "We go for our country and Union, and for brave little Jessie forever."

Frémont's supporters did everything they could to "use" Jessie, and at times it seemed as if she was the candidate, and not he. This proved to be a detriment to the campaign on one occasion in New Hampshire. With a poster proclaiming "John and Jessie" and another urging "Jessie for the White House," a local newspaper concluded that Jessie was trying to promote the rights of women while campaigning for her husband. Later in her life she did support women's issues, albeit quietly—but for now, her goal was to see her husband elected president of the United States.

For a while, there seemed a real possibility that Frémont would make it, that he just might become president. He had

Postcard mailed by the Frémont campaign to take advantage of Jessie's popularity. When a tab at the bottom is pulled down, the character's face changes from delight to anger. The face showing displeasure over Jessie's work in Pennsylvania was needless, as Frémont lost the election because he failed to carry Buchanan's home state. (Frémont Letters and Papers, James S. Copley Library)

skilled political managers on his side, in addition to most of the powerful northern newspapers. And, of course, he had Jessie. She appeared at rallies, helped organize campaign literature, met with advisors, and continued to protect her husband as best she could from continuing attacks by his opponents. Such exertion taxed her strength and she tried to cut down on her activities, but she could not. All of this effort, however, was not rewarded. John Charles Frémont did not become the first elected Republican president of the United States. That honor was to be Abraham Lincoln's, four years later. In an odd twist, there was a movement before Frémont's campaign began to have Lincoln be his running mate, but it was organized too late for that to happen. Instead, William L. Dayton, a former U.S. senator from New Jersey, was the vice presidential candidate. The paths of Lincoln and Frémont would cross again just a few years later. For now, Frémont lost to Buchanan, despite carrying eleven of the sixteen northern states.

It was a close election, with Buchanan receiving 1.5 million of the popular vote while almost 1.4 million cast their ballots for Frémont. It was Buchanan's home state of Pennsylvania that provided him with the winning margin in the electoral college. The majority of electoral votes needed for victory was 149 out of a possible 296. Prior to winning Pennsylvania's 27 votes, Buchanan had 147 electors. He won the presidency with a total of 174 electoral votes compared to Frémont's 114. The remaining 8 votes went to a third-party candidate, Millard Fillmore. If no candidate had obtained enough votes, the election would have gone to the House of Representatives for a decision, as required by the U.S. Constitution. The Buchanan victory avoided a constitutional crisis.

According to various accounts, the Frémonts took the loss as well as anyone could after such a heated contest. Lily wrote that her "father took the defeat calmly, cheerfully bowing to the will of the majority." Jessie, always the competitor, was terribly disappointed but presented a strong front. Only fourteen-year-old Lily displayed her emotion by shedding copious tears until her mother told her to stop and go for a long walk!

What might have happened if Frémont had won—could civil war have been averted? In his biography of Frémont, Allan Nevins writes: "Historians of the period, almost without exception, have declared it fortunate that Frémont was not elected and that the United States did not have to face the possible ordeal of civil war under a head so inexperienced, so rash and impetuous, so brilliantly erratic." One has to wonder if this argument can be extended to Jessie, because she and Frémont were so close and because when the American Civil War did come, they together did something "so rash and impetuous" that it caused great anxiety and distress to President Lincoln. But all of this was a few years away.

In the spring of 1857, Jessie, John, and the children sailed for Europe to heal their collective wounds and visit with friends and members of Jessie's family. Frémont did not stay away from the United States for long; he soon returned to California to attend to his mining interests. While in Paris, Jessie received word that her father was ill, and she immediately returned to Washington. Frémont joined her there, and the family lived in the nation's capital during the winter of 1857–1858 so that Jessie could be near her father.

When difficulties arose with his Mariposa mines again, Frémont was called back to California. Jessie soon followed. On April 10, 1858, two days before she and the children reached San Francisco, Sen. Thomas Hart Benton died in his home in Washington. He was seventy-six years old. A train took his body back west to St. Louis for burial in the historic Bellafontaine Cemetery, where he was laid next to his wife, Elizabeth. Jessie took the loss of her father hard, her grief profound. Before long, however, there would be other turmoil to face, both personal and national. How would Jessie confront these two challenges?

CHAPTER 7

Turmoil

With the death of her father, Jessie accepted California as her home. She remarked in *Souvenirs* that California had provided her with "wealth and honors. There was my home. There was my future. When the death of my parents left me no divided feeling I no longer looked back." Jessie worked to turn the Frémonts' Las Mariposas ranch into a comfortable dwelling. She added fireplaces to the structure, had it painted and wallpapered, and brought furniture and other household furnishings from San Francisco. She had the help of a maid and a cook from France. In her *Recollections,* Lily recalled, "We felt that we had a real home in the wilderness."

The Mariposa mines were the source of the money that enabled these expenditures, but the mines also required a great amount of attention and money to operate. Legal matters required attention as well. Like all other land grants from the Mexican era, the Frémonts' land title had to be validated by the proper authorities in the State of California. The Frémonts complied with this law.

The gold fields, though, were areas of constant lawlessness. By California law, squatters could take over any mines that they believed had been vacated or were unoccupied. As Jessie explained in *Far-West Sketches,* the law was poorly written: "All the trouble arose from the construction of that word, 'unoccupied.' A small miner working alone would go to dinner, and immediately men watching for the chance would seize and hold against him his lawful property." Lily related, "My father lost the Black Drift

Mine under the law, the guard left at the mine having been bribed to leave it long enough for another to take possession." According to Allan Nevins, Jessie "knew nothing of business accounts and of squatter turbulence," leaving those matters to her husband. In the summer of 1858, though, one armed and dangerous attempt did catch her attention.

A group of men tried to seize Frémont's Pine Tree Mine, thinking it was unoccupied, but found six of Frémont's employees working deep inside the mineshaft. The invaders demanded that they leave, but the workers refused. As a consequence, the claim-jumpers tried to starve the mineworkers out by not allowing them to have any food or water. Over the course of five days, the force of squatters grew to about a hundred, with Frémont's forces numbering twenty-seven. The situation escalated when the wife of one of the miners being held hostage attempted to take charge. Jessie described in *Sketches* what happened:

> She made her way through the packed crowd, a little creature but a great heart, carrying a big basket of provisions and—a revolver. Her finger was on the trigger as she pushed forward.
>
> "I shoot the first man that hinders me. You wouldn't like to be shot by a woman! But I'll shoot to kill. You've just got to let me carry his supper in to Caton. You have your quarrel with the Colonel [Frémont] about mines and lands and you can fight that out with him. But I'm a poor woman that's got only my husband—and five children for him to work for. You sha'n't take his life for your quarrels! He's only doing his duty."
>
> And with her uplifted revolver waving like a fan towards one and then another, they fell back and let her enter the mine— some laughing, some praising her, some swearing at her. She carried not only food but ammunition; and three revolvers hung from her waist under her skirts.

This show of bravado was not enough, though, to end the stand-off. Jessie became involved in the situation, as Lily detailed: "A written notice was served upon us, in which we were told that the men were 'bound to have their rights,' . . .

otherwise they would burn the house over our heads and then the Colonel would be killed." Jessie managed to control the problem:

> [She told] the writers of that message that the house and land was ours, and that we intended to remain upon it. "If the house is burned," she said, "we will camp on the land, and if the men kill the Colonel as threatened, then we will sell the property to a corporation that is anxious to buy it, and the property will come under the control of men who will be much harder to deal with than Colonel Frémont."

The trouble was eventually defused when a contingent of men from the governor's office arrived in response to a plea for help from Frémont's supporters. The Mariposa mines remained in Frémont's control, and once again Jessie was at the forefront in "rescuing" her husband—a role she seemed to continually play.

During their time at the ranch, Jessie and the children sometimes traveled three thousand feet up the nearby mountain range for camping trips to escape the intolerable heat of their Bear Valley home. Frémont joined them, but went down the mountain daily to conduct business affairs connected with his gold mines and lumber mills, rejoining his family at night. For her part, Jessie kept busy: she schooled her children, read to them, and rode through the mountains with them, exploring the beauty of their surroundings. These camping trips were not long enough for Jessie, and she often journeyed to cooler San Francisco for relief from the great warmth of California's central valley region. "At Bear Valley," Lily wrote, "my mother was like an exile, for she was not interested in mines, horses, or chickens, but she cheerfully made the best of conditions and never complained." However, the heat and lack of social opportunities got the best of her, and in 1859 Frémont purchased, for $42,000, a twelve-acre plot of land in San Francisco. It was on the water, overlooking Alcatraz Island, and it had "a tiny cottage built on the edge of the bluff, on a small point projecting out into the

Jessie sitting on the porch of her home, Black Point, in San Francisco. Jessie loved this house, with its spectacular view of California's famous bay, and she liked hosting social gatherings and sharing it with others. (Bancroft Library)

Bay." Jessie immediately fell in love with it and the Frémonts named it Black Point, but they called it home for only a few years. During the Civil War, the government seized the property for coastline fortification, never paying the Frémonts for it, even after the war was over.

While Jessie was happy at Black Point, Frémont was having trouble with his mines at Mariposa. They were producing good amounts of ore and income, but improvements to them were necessary for better and more efficient production. All of this was expensive, and Frémont did not have the money available to make such upgrades since he had not wisely managed the

John Charles Frémont as he appeared upon assuming command of the Western Department in 1861. (Frémont Letters and Papers, James S. Copley Library)

substantial income he received from his investments. Therefore, in early 1861, he traveled to Europe to seek financial support for his properties and to help retire the debts he had incurred. On April 13, while he was abroad, South Carolina shore batteries fired upon Fort Sumter, a Union garrison in Charleston's harbor, and the American Civil War began.

Having a premonition that events would take a turn in that direction, he had written Jessie that if and when a war started, she should make her way to New York and meet him there. He booked passage as soon as he could for the United States, but Jessie's trip east was delayed by a carriage accident and it was a few weeks before she could travel. When she was able to make the trip, she rented out the house at Black Point and boarded a steamer with her children. When their ship tied up at a wharf in New York, they found Frémont waiting for them. He told them they were heading west—he had been given a military command.

The hot, war-torn summer of 1861 found John Charles Frémont in Missouri. President Lincoln appointed him commander of the Department of the West, which included Illinois and all the states and territories from the Mississippi River to the Rocky Mountains. Headquarters for the department was in St. Louis. Frémont and Jessie arrived there by train on July 25, 1861, after he had spent several weeks in New York dealing with personal business matters.

Many thought that Frémont's talents were not up to the job. This was going to be a difficult billet. Lincoln expected Frémont to bring calm to the violence that was erupting across Missouri. Michael Fellman, author of *Inside War: The Guerrilla Conflict in Missouri during the American Civil War*, states the problem that confronted both Lincoln and Frémont: "Lincoln knew that only a general who was a masterful actor could maneuver successfully among strife-torn Missouri [factions]. . . . With many of its citizens sympathetic to the South, many more neutralist, and almost none Republican, Missouri institutions replicated th[e] shattered polity [of the nation]."

The Southern Confederacy hoped to persuade Missouri to join its cause. But Lincoln desperately needed to hold onto the border slave states of Kentucky, Maryland, Delaware, and Missouri if the Union was to have a chance of prevailing. With about 68,000 square miles and a population of around a million, it was crucial that Missouri remain on the Northern side. This was to be Frémont's primary goal, and it would not be an easy one to achieve. Given its size and history, with both pro- and antislavery factions active in the state, Missouri would become a battleground unto itself.

Frémont's task was daunting. To start with, the St. Louis that he and Jessie knew and loved had changed dramatically. She described it this way in *Souvenirs*:

Everything changed. There was no life on the river; the many steamboats were laid up at their wharves, their fires out, the singing, cheery crews gone—they, empty, swaying idly with the current. As we drove through the deserted streets we saw only closed shutters to warehouses and business places; the wheels and the horses' hoofs echoed loud and harsh as when one drives through the silent streets late in the night.

It was a hostile city and showed itself as such.

A curfew had been declared, troops drilled in the streets, and the city was torn apart by conflicting allegiances. St. Louis was not a happy place to be, nor for that matter was the entire state of Missouri. It was as if there were two civil wars being waged: one national and one regional.

By the time Frémont arrived in St. Louis to assume command, Missouri was in a state of insurrection. Events had begun to spiral downward when Claiborne F. Jackson, a long-time slave owner and surreptitious supporter of the Confederacy, became governor. At his inauguration on January 3, 1861, Jackson seemingly declared his support for the Union, but, as noted by the authors of *Missouri: The Heart of the Nation,* he also made his pro-Southern sympathies known, "declaring that [the Union] must ensure equality for both Northern and Southern states where slavery in the territories was concerned. The North had brought the nation to this crisis by its seeming unwillingness to accept such a principle." Jackson declared that Missouri would go its own way—his way, the way of the South, to the Confederacy.

Perhaps the best assessment of how the citizens of Missouri felt about the coming conflict and the split it would cause can be found in Richard S. Brownlee's book, *Gray Ghosts of the Confederacy:*

At the advent of the Civil War Missouri was still largely a frontier state—a Southern frontier state. In 1860 some three quarters of the people had their origin in or were descended from parents who were born in other slave states. Thus they were of decided

The St. Louis headquarters where Jessie and her husband resided during his tenure as commander of the Western Department. The mansion belonged to a cousin of Jessie's, Col. J. B. Brant, who insisted that the Frémonts use it both for military and personal needs, and they were criticized for living in a lavish manner during the Civil War. The government was said to have paid Brant $6,000 annually for the use of the estate, which only added to the image of a sumptuous lifestyle. (State Historical Society of Missouri, Columbia)

Southern background and many of them had family ties and cultural affiliation with the old border states. By 1860 slaves made up only about nine per cent of the population of Missouri, but the institution was still an important factor in the agricultural economy and was increasing in the rich farm lands of the central and western portion of the state. There were few large slaveholders, but a great many men owned one or two Negroes who were valuable personal property, indicative of wealth and in some cases advanced social status. Since Missouri's admission to the Union slavery had been inextricably bound to other social institutions and was taken for granted by most men.

Like the nation, Missourians split over the issue of slavery; not all citizens agreed with their governor. Anxiety increased in Missouri between the time of Jackson's swearing in and the fall of Fort Sumter, as factions on both sides of the slavery issue intensified their rhetoric and actions. Brownlee elaborates on the schizophrenic nature of the problem:

> The most important fact was that many men of Southern origin were simply unwilling to engage in a war against the Union. The wealthier class of slaveholders, it may be presumed, was not so foolish as to trust their lives or property to the Confederacy with the state firmly in the hands of Union military forces. As long as the western border and Missouri remained tranquil, as long as the abolition of slavery was not a primary issue in the war, as long as men of Southern background and origin would be recognized in their loyalty to the Union and were able to conduct their lives and affairs in normal peace and security, there was little reason for serious strife.

These were Lincoln's sentiments and goals, yet no matter how you looked at it, a confrontation was brewing for the state of Missouri: Unionists formed paramilitary Home Guard units and Confederate supporters plotted to have Missouri leave the Union. The clash came on May 10, 1861, in what came to be known as the Camp Jackson Affair.

Nathaniel Lyon was involved in the Camp Jackson Affair and fought in other military campaigns in Missouri. His death at Wilson's Creek made him a war hero and an idol of Union supporters. (*Abraham Lincoln: A History*, James S. Copley Library)

It began with a State Guard encampment in St. Louis named after Governor Jackson. The purpose of the camp was supposedly to drill and prepare troops so that Missouri could protect itself if necessary. In reality, while there were Unionists among those at the garrison, the governor was seeking help in the form of arms and ammunition from Jefferson Davis, president of the Confederacy. In *Frank Blair: Lincoln's Conservative*, William E. Parrish writes that Davis was more than willing to help. However, he wanted something in return: "a Missouri regiment for service in Virginia, something that Jackson had to decline for the moment." Clearly, Missouri, and St. Louis in particular, was fast becoming a political battleground in the Civil War.

Local Union Safety Committee members learned of Davis's

As Lyon and his troops marched their prisoners from Camp Jackson to the St. Louis Arsenal, a mob attacked them and a riot ensued. (State Historical Society of Missouri, Columbia)

desire to aid Jackson's supporters and they also knew of a shipment of munitions that arrived in St. Louis early on May 9 from an arsenal in Baton Rouge, Louisiana. Parrish details what was in that consignment: "two twelve-pound howitzers, two thirty-two pound siege guns, five hundred muskets, and a large amount of ammunition." Committee members let the delivery pass, unchallenged, on its way to Camp Jackson. Capt. Nathaniel Lyon, the military leader of the Home Guards, visited Camp Jackson in disguise to scrutinize the stronghold later in the day. He found that reports of the arms buildup were indeed accurate and he determined that the encampment must be taken. His troops, composed primarily of German immigrants who were loyal to the Union, moved on Camp Jackson the following day, May 10. The garrison surrendered peaceably. However, trouble ensued as the prisoners were being transferred to the U.S. arsenal for processing.

As Lyon's troops marched the captives to the arsenal, a crowd gathered, some with guns, some shouting support for the Confederacy and Davis. To this day, no one knows how the scuffle started, but soon the mob became angry and ugly, shouting and throwing objects at the tramping soldiers and their detainees. Shots rang out. When the dust cleared, twenty-eight people had died. The following day, the Camp Jackson prisoners were paroled, but in the aftermath Lyon took his men to Jefferson City to hold the capitol and subsequently defeated State Guard troops in the Battle of Boonville. Governor Jackson fled south, seeking sanctuary and continuing to engage in activities to bring Missouri into the Confederacy, which did nothing to calm the upheaval sweeping the state. A new pro-Union provisional governor, Hamilton R. Gamble, took office, but the situation continued to deteriorate.

This was the chaotic state of affairs that Frémont and Jessie found when they arrived in St. Louis on July 25. Escalating the grim circumstances, Jackson issued a proclamation from New Madrid on August 5 declaring Missouri an independent and sovereign state. This was an obvious preparation for the state's joining the Confederacy, challenging both Governor Gamble's and General Frémont's authority. The turmoil continued, and several days later, on August 10, a battle ensued at Wilson's Creek near Springfield. According to the authors of *Missouri: The Heart of the Nation*, Lyon, now a general, "called for reinforcements which Frémont felt he could not spare. . . . He ordered Lyon to retreat." Frémont believed that Lyon underestimated the force he faced, and wrote him that he should fall back and wait for reinforcements at Rolla if he thought he could not maintain his position. Lyon refused to retreat, following a plan presented to him by Gen. Franz Sigel, a leader of German volunteers. Ferocious combat resulted and Lyon lost his life. The victory belonged to the Southern faction, but they could not take advantage of their success because of heavy losses and lack of arms.

Jackson continued his efforts to have Missouri become part of the Confederacy up until his death in December 1862 in Arkansas.

More important, violence intensified in Missouri. As John G. Nicolay and John Hay, two of Lincoln's secretaries, wrote in *Abraham Lincoln: A History*, "There broke out in many parts of the State a destructive guerrilla warfare, degenerating into neighborhood and family feuds and bloody personal reprisal and revenge, which became known under the term of 'bushwhacking.' Houses and bridges were burned, farms were plundered, railroads were obstructed and broken, men were kidnapped and assassinated." Throughout Missouri, according to Nicolay and Hay, "disorder, lawlessness, crime, and almost anarchy" prevailed, with no way to suppress such activities—it seemed as if the advocates of both sides, pro- and anti-Union, ran unchecked. This was the chaos that awaited Frémont. Lincoln and the country were counting on him to take charge and bring some measure of control back to Missouri. He tried, but in the end he failed.

Frémont quickly sent troops to areas of unrest in an attempt to impose order, declared martial law in the city of St. Louis, soon extending it throughout the state, and began building defenses around municipalities like Rolla and Jefferson City that were vulnerable to attack. These were the easy decisions to make—they were obvious. There were harder choices that had to be made, such as what methods to use in prosecuting the war in Missouri. Carl Sandburg, in his book *Abraham Lincoln: The War Years*, wrote that Frémont surrounded himself with "dapper foreigners, trained in European tactics and methods, [who] were to assist him in solving civil war in the State of Missouri." These Frémont associates gave themselves grand-sounding titles that put people off. In addition, Frémont located his headquarters in an opulent mansion belonging to Jessie's cousin that sent the wrong impression: that he and Jessie were living well while the rest of Missouri was in turmoil. Sandburg stated: "He could handle outfits of one or two hundred men on the plains or desert or in unexplored mountains. Riding the human whirlwind in Missouri was another affair."

And there was more. When it came to administrative duties,

Frémont fared no better. As is normal in any wartime situation, there was discontent with how appointments, commissions, and contracts were awarded. However, Frémont showed no common sense when it came to these matters, and bitter disappointments occurred, as Nicolay and Hay explained: "Instead of bringing order into the chaotic condition of military business, he was prone to set method and routine at defiance, issuing commissions and directing the giving out of contracts in so irregular a way as to bring a protest from the proper accounting officers of the Government." There were even rumors that he was thinking of establishing an "independent dictatorship in the West." The situation was not going well and would soon get worse.

Frémont was in over his head. He apparently could not handle the state of affairs he was entrusted with; he could not end the lawlessness that was plaguing Missouri. Lincoln was beginning to take notice of the disorder and he began quickly losing confidence in his Western Commander. Sandburg summed it up: "The defect in Frémont was that he was a dreamer. . . impractical. . . a poor judge of men and formed strange associations. He surrounded himself with foreigners . . . most of whom were adventurers [or] swindlers." In Frémont's defense, it should be noted that he complained he did not have enough manpower, but department commanders always want more troops.

As if all of this ineptness was not enough, Frémont then did something that deeply angered Lincoln: he attempted to free the slaves of Missouri. It was an act that could have altered the course of the Civil War and possibly caused the Union to lose the conflict. Frémont, a military man who could not handle what had been given him, turned to an area that he was not authorized to deal with—setting wartime policy goals and objectives. His efforts backfired and caused a tremendous uproar that was felt all the way from St. Louis to Washington, D.C. To help in the damage control that was necessary because of his action, Frémont turned to the one person who always was ready to defend him, whether he was right or wrong—he turned to Jessie to argue his case before the president of the United States.

CHAPTER 8

Jessie and Lincoln

On August 30, 1861, Major General John Charles Frémont took a step that placed him in direct opposition to his commander-in-chief, Abraham Lincoln. That morning, after giving it careful thought the previous night, Frémont issued a proclamation declaring martial law throughout Missouri, an action that the president had not authorized. In addition, the proclamation declared free all slaves in the state whose owners had taken up arms against the Union. The general's action alarmed not only the president and Missouri state officials, but the governors of the other border states as well.

Frémont said his reason for issuing the proclamation was to bring law and order to the state of Missouri. In addition to declaring martial law, the proclamation stated that "all persons who shall be taken with arms in their hand within these lines, shall be tried by court-martial, and if found guilty, will be shot." Property, including "chattel," of those Missourians or others fighting in the state against the Union—and there were thousands doing that—would be "confiscated to the public use; and their slaves, if any they have, are hereby declared free." What was set free instead was a firestorm. Frémont had not conferred with the president. In fact, he had told only Jessie and a close aide about the proclamation, a few hours before it was publicly announced. Jessie, an antislavery advocate, totally agreed with her husband's measure. It was good that she did, because she would soon have to defend his actions in Washington, D.C., to President Lincoln.

This portrait of Abraham Lincoln, the sixteenth president of the United States, was painted by William Cogswell after the president's death and is unusual because it shows him standing. Most often seen are busts of President Lincoln or paintings and photographs showing him seated. *(White House Gallery of Official Portraits of the Presidents,* James S. Copley Library)

The president, like the nation as a whole, was astounded by Frémont's edict. Since winning the 1860 election and assuming the presidency, Lincoln had tried his utmost to avoid civil war. But once it was a reality, he knew that if the Union were to have a chance of survival, the border states that permitted slavery— Missouri, Kentucky, Maryland, and Delaware—had to remain loyal. These states controlled vital waterways capable of moving men, equipment, and products that were essential to the Union's cause. Lincoln knew full well that there were Southern sympathizers in each of the border states and that the Confederates wanted to persuade as many of those states as they could to join their rebellion. If they were successful, it could be a prelude to toppling the Union. Keeping these states satisfied, Lincoln thought, could keep them from joining the South. He therefore did his very best to avoid the appearance of threatening slavery where it existed. The one thing Lincoln did not want to do was to tamper with the "peculiar institution" as it existed in the border states. At the same time, he had to deal with those in the North who wanted to make slavery the central issue in the war. For Lincoln, the objective had always been the preservation of the Union, the very reason for the war. Nothing was more important in his mind or in his policy.

The president was walking a fine line. It was not that he was proslavery. He had won election on a Republican Party platform opposing the extension of slavery into the western territories. He was not an abolitionist either—he knew that America could not exist "half slave and half free," but he believed that it was not the right time to be pushing the issue as Frémont did. On September 22, 1862, Lincoln issued his own Emancipation Proclamation, which took effect a hundred days later on January 1, 1863. Always aware of the sensitivity of the slavery issue, he did not force emancipation upon the border states even then. He offered the rebellious states the opportunity to keep their "chattel" if they stopped fighting. The document said: "That on the 1st day of January, A.D. 1863, all persons held as slaves within any State or designated part of a State the people whereof shall then be in rebellion against the United States shall be then, thenceforward, and forever free."

In this statement, Lincoln did not tamper with the institution of slavery. To the contrary, he told the Southern states that had left the Union that if they rejoined the Union by January 1, 1863, they could keep their slaves, because they would no longer "be in rebellion against the United States." The border states, like Missouri, had nothing to fear from Lincoln's proclamation, because they were never in rebellion against the United States. He was not trying to take away their "property," as Frémont had attempted to do. In truth, the president was attempting a political ploy. He hoped to divide the Confederacy by tempting mutinous states to break with the Southern cause, using slavery as a carrot: come back into the Union and you can keep your slaves. If the maneuver had worked, the war might have ended earlier. But it did not work, and the war dragged on for two more years. Lincoln's edict did not free slaves in any state, rebellious or not.

Frémont prematurely forced Lincoln's hand. His proclamation could cause Missouri and the other border states to flee the Union and seek a haven in the Southern Confederacy. If this happened, all of Lincoln's hard work in the border states would be for naught. In his book *Lincoln*, David Herbert Donald provides a glimpse into the president's thinking. He writes: "Lincoln would not permit civilian authority to be overruled by the military, and he would not allow sensitive questions concerning slavery and emancipation to be decided by anyone but the President himself." The author cites Lincoln as writing that Frémont's action was "*purely political* and not within the range of *military* law, or necessity." Donald goes on to say, "It was, in fact, simply dictatorship, because it assumed 'that the general may do *anything* he pleases.'" This was just the latest issue that caused the president to be concerned about Frémont. Donald continues:

> The general, who had made his reputation as a pathmarker of the Western trails to California, was never able to find his way across the Missouri political terrain. He quarreled with everybody. He scorned the duly elected, if ineffectual, governor of Missouri, Hamilton R. Gamble, who promptly went to Washington with complaints about military incompetence in St. Louis. He quarreled with his subordinates.

Lincoln's immediate concern was to procure a copy of Frémont's proclamation; he did not want to rely on newspaper accounts. Once he had read it, he dispatched a letter by special messenger to Frémont in St. Louis. In it, he warned Frémont that "the confiscation of property and the liberating slaves of traitorous owners, will alarm our Southern Union friends and turn them against us." As always, Lincoln was looking at the big picture: his object was to save the Union. If Frémont's unautho-

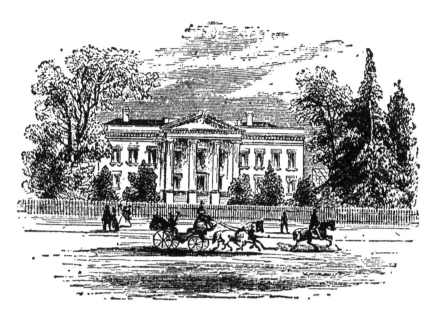

The White House as it looked when Jessie visited President Lincoln there in 1861. (*Abraham Lincoln: The War Years,* James S. Copley Library)

rized declaration was allowed to stand, border states such as Missouri, Kentucky, and Maryland might abandon Lincoln's fragile alliance of loyal Union states, and that could spell the end of the Union. With this in mind, the president asked his major general to "modify that paragraph" of the edict that was troublesome. He concluded by telling Frémont that he wrote to him in the "spirit of caution, and not censure."

Frémont was in no mood to reconcile. In his reply to the president, he stubbornly clung to the notion that if he was "to retract [my proclamation] of my own accord, it would imply that I myself thought it wrong, and that I had acted without the reflection which the gravity of the point demanded." Denying Lincoln's polite request, he wrote: "I have to ask that you will openly direct me to make the correction." Frémont did not want to look foolish, but he apparently was not concerned that Lincoln would. No matter his feelings about slavery, Frémont's position was untenable. He decided to send Jessie to Washington with his response and to argue the cause he felt so deeply about. It was typical of him that he would not go himself, but instead send his wife. He and Jessie thought that if she went to the White House and met with Lincoln in person she could persuade him to come around to their way of thinking. They were wrong.

By again ignoring the president's wishes and publicly challenging Lincoln to force him to rescind his edict, Frémont only made matters worse. The nation watched, waited, and wondered how Lincoln would deal with Frémont. The commander of the western division had committed an act of insubordination against his commander-in-chief. He had rejected all appropriate channels and sidestepped the proper chain of command. What would Lincoln do?

An angry and upset Jessie left St. Louis on September 8, 1861. She took with her Frémont's letter and her English maid. On her way, Jessie must have been thinking of the previous time she had gone to plead her husband's case before a president of the United States—when she and Kit Carson went to President Polk to try to spare Frémont the indignity of a court-martial. Her efforts had failed then; certainly she hoped she would be more successful this time. The train trip to the nation's capital took two days and the cars were stifling, packed with civilians and military personnel. There were no private compartments available, so Jessie sat in her seat for the entire trip. She arrived in Washington hot, grimy, and exhausted but determined to get Lincoln to see her husband's point of view.

Jessie went straight to the Willard Hotel to meet some friends and, hopefully, to get some rest and change her clothes before meeting with the president. She sent a note to Lincoln asking when she could meet with him. He replied: "Now, at once." It was late in the evening, almost midnight, when Jessie and a friend walked over to the White House.

Jessie wrote about her meeting with Lincoln, and her account found its way into many works of American history, including Allan Nevins's book on Frémont: "We were asked into the usual receiving room, the red room, next to the large dining room.

Photograph of the Willard Hotel, from which Lincoln summoned Jessie for their critical meeting. Over the years it became the preferred place for politicians, writers, businessmen, and ordinary Americans to stay. Within walking distance of the White House, the hotel still attracts Washington society today. *(Abraham Lincoln: The War Years,* James S. Copley Library)

After some little waiting the President came in from that dining room." Jessie introduced her friend, who then stepped aside so that she and Lincoln could talk. She recalled: "The President's manner . . . was hard. Nor did he offer me a seat. He talked standing, and both voice and manner made the impression that I was to be got rid of briefly." The president said, "Well?" Jessie handed him Frémont's letter. As he read it, Jessie found a chair, and when he finished his reading, he sat beside her. She explained that Frémont placed great importance on the letter and wanted to make sure that it reached Lincoln and had his undivided attention. Thus, they had both decided that she should deliver it in person. "He answered, not to that, but to the subject his own mind was upon, that 'It was a war for a great national idea, the Union, and that General Frémont should not have dragged the Negro into it.'"

Jessie continued promoting her husband's ideas, expressing the notion that the war might not be won by "arms alone." Lincoln said that he already had written to Frémont about what he wanted him to do, not waiting for Jessie to bring him the letter. Jessie skirted this information and kept on chatting, taking the opportunity to further her husband's case. She said that the general "thought it would be well if Mr. Lincoln explained personally his ideas and desires," because he felt he was at a "great disadvantage of being perhaps opposed by people in whom you [Lincoln] have every confidence."

The "people" Jessie was referring to were members of the Blair family, prominent Washington figures with political ties to Missouri. Francis Preston Blair was an influential newspaper editor who had become an adviser to Lincoln. His son Frank Blair, Jr., a Missouri congressman, had once been a close friend and supporter of Frémont. As a colonel in the Union army, Frank Blair had promoted Frémont's appointment as major general and head of the Western Department, and he was sympathetic to Frémont's pleas for more troops to confront the havoc in Missouri. However, over time Frank Blair came to believe, as others did, that Frémont did not have the ability to lead. His relationship with the general and Jessie turned acrimonious as business and political wrangling increased.

Jessie and members of the Blair family had been close correspondents, but by now the Blairs were fierce Frémont detractors. Jessie thought that the Blairs and their friends were behind all her husband's problems; after all, they had the ear of the president. Lincoln denied any such thing. Neither Jessie nor her husband ever considered that Frémont, so strident in his views, might have some culpability in the matter.

It was people like the Blairs, and their anti-Frémont stance, that Jessie wanted to make the issue in her conversation with Lincoln. He was a bit surprised by her boldness, and as Jessie was leaving he said, "You are quite a female politician." Instead of taking this remark as a compliment, Jessie thought Lincoln was being dismissive of her because she was a woman. Their meeting was over, and Jessie returned to her hotel.

Lincoln's impression of the meeting was not very different from Jessie's. John G. Nicolay and John Hay, in their work on Lincoln, include his notes: "Mrs. Frémont, coming to see me. She sought an audience with me at midnight, and taxed me so violently with many things that I had to exercise all the awkward tact I have to avoid quarreling with her."

The dispatch that Lincoln had sent to Frémont before Jessie's arrival was blunt, leaving no doubt of what he wanted his major general to do. It stated: "The particular clause, however, in relation to the confiscation of property and the liberation of slaves appeared to me to be objectionable." Lincoln went on to cite Frémont's demand that "I should make an open order for the modification, which I very cheerfully do. It is therefore ordered that the said clause of said proclamation be so modified." And so it was done; Lincoln rescinded the order and Frémont's emancipation fiasco was over.

In an ironic twist of fate, given all that happened, Missouri actually abolished slavery before the adoption of the constitutional amendment freeing the slaves. On January 6, 1865, three months before the Civil War officially ended and almost a year before the adoption of the Thirteenth Amendment on December 6, Missouri authorities convened a constitutional convention in Mercantile Hall, St. Louis. Five days later, the convention passed "An Ordinance Abolishing Slavery in Missouri," which clearly stated: "That hereafter in this State there shall be neither Slavery nor involuntary Servitude, except in punishment of crime . . . and all persons held to Service or labor as slaves, are hereby declared free." This ordinance, which took effect immediately, did what Frémont could not do and what America succeeded in doing only after the bloody national conflict was over.

Jessie returned to St. Louis with bitterness toward the president and the Blairs, whom she saw as guilty of betrayal. So deep was the chasm between the once close friends that Jessie led her

A rendering of Col. Frank Blair based on a portrait by the famed Civil War photographer Mathew Brady. (State Historical Society of Missouri, Columbia)

husband to issue a warrant for Frank Blair's arrest. According to Blair's biographer William E. Parrish, she "spewed out her new-found hatred of the Blairs to her husband," and on September 16, 1861, Frémont ordered the "arrest of Frank Blair because of his 'insidious & dishonorable efforts to bring my authority into contempt with the Government.'" Blair was arrested, but released. The controversy continued, and Blair was rearrested and held in Jefferson Barracks near St. Louis until General of the Army Winfield Scott ordered him freed. Parrish writes: "Jessie's visit to the capital marked the decisive turning point in the relationship between the two families. Always defensive in support of her husband, she overreacted, out of ignorance and suspicion, to what she considered unjust attacks on his motives." There is no doubt that Jessie was a vocal cheerleader for her husband and all that he did, just as there is no doubt that Frémont had limited command experience and was unable to handle the situation in Missouri.

Frémont's military assignment now appeared to be in jeopardy. The only hope of salvaging his billet would be some sort of victory in battle. With that in mind, Frémont led his men into the fray. Jessie and other officers' wives traveled to Jefferson City near the end of September to bid farewell to their husbands and offer good wishes to the troops. Frémont and his forces were about to venture off in pursuit of armed Confederate sympathizers under the command of Gen. Sterling Price, a former governor of Missouri with pro-Southern sympathies who had fought against Lyon's troops at Wilson's Creek.

Many in Frémont's command thought that his troops were not ready for battle, lacking proper equipment and food supplies. Frémont forged ahead anyway and had some success in a battle near Springfield that led to his occupation of the town. Time had run out for him, however. A dispatch from President Lincoln arrived on November 3, 1861, while Frémont was in the field. He was relieved of command. The order was issued on October 24, but it had taken time to reach him. Frémont had been commander of the Western Department for just three months.

Nicolay and Hay sum it up: "In his brief incumbency he not only lost the general public confidence, but incurred the special displeasure or direct enmity of those most prominent in influence or command next to him, and without whose friendship and cooperation success was practically impossible." In short, Frémont failed his opportunity at an important military posting. He was good at exploring western lands, but lacked the ability to oversee a large contingent of men.

There was more to this situation, though, than Frémont's lack of ability to lead in wartime. He and Jessie were favorites of the American abolitionist movement, and they had their own agenda—freeing the slaves was important to them. When their ideas were not welcomed, they saw those who were out to thwart them as conspirators. Lincoln took a broader view. He was committed to preserving the Union at all costs. In the summer of 1861, though, slavery was a divisive issue, and in truth it always would be. Frémont and Jessie could not see the bigger picture and so Frémont had to go. In the U.S. military there is only one ultimate commander, and that is the president of the United

States. Throughout the country's history, adherence to this principle makes the chain of command work, for good or ill.

Jessie and John took the children and left St. Louis by the end of November, angry and resentful. Frémont received a rousing send-off from his troops. There was no way of knowing that he would have yet another chance to prove that he could command men during a time of war and not just on peaceful western expeditions. For now, the Frémonts journeyed to New York to wait for whatever the future held.

CHAPTER 9

The Frémonts ~ The Later Years

$\mathcal{A}$fter being relieved of the western command and returning with his family to their home in New York City, Frémont sulked at the turn of events. As for Jessie, her anger was deep, but she channeled her disappointment and frustration into writing a book about the Missouri troops called *The Story of the Guard: A Chronicle of the War*. All profits from this popular account went to charity. Frémont's brooding soon ended, because the radical wing of the president's party believed in him and in his antislavery stance. The Radicals exerted pressure on Lincoln, and Frémont was chosen in March 1862 to lead the newly formed Mountain Department, which included parts of Kentucky, Tennessee, and Virginia. The headquarters were located in Wheeling, West Virginia.

Jessie and the children went with Frémont to his new assignment, but they remained there only a month before returning to New York. Frémont's stay was not much longer, because his experience with this assignment was as distressful as his time in Missouri. Shortly after Frémont assumed control of the Mountain Department, Lincoln and the War Department reorganized the structure of the military command to meet wartime needs. Frémont was not happy—he did not like his new superior officer, John Pope, with whom he had had disagreements when they both were in Missouri. Protesting the changes, he resigned his position in June 1862, having served less than four months, a little longer than he had served in Missouri. Once more Frémont was a military officer without a command during a tumultuous time in American history. He returned to his family in New York.

All the hopes, all the dreams, all the aspirations that Jessie had for her husband, all the plans for a distinguished career and life modeled after that of her father, were now gone. Once more Frémont brooded and Jessie became bitter, believing that he had not been given a fair chance at proving himself as a military leader in time of war. She blamed Lincoln, his advisors, and her former friends for engaging in political intrigue, backstabbing, and betrayal. Never once did she seem to consider that her husband might have some responsibility for his predicament. She needed the skills and reputation of her father to smooth over the rough spots for Frémont—Senator Benton would have done that for his son-in-law, as he had in the past, but he was gone. Jessie could not do it by herself; she had neither the proper connections nor the political skill. She had used up any goodwill she might have had when she confronted President Lincoln in a situation that ended in a debacle. Resentment would soon give way to other concerns, however.

While in the military, Frémont paid little or no attention to his personal business affairs, and his failure to do so was costly. The mines at Mariposa had always been difficult to run at a consistent profit, and Frémont was not a good businessman—he was constantly trying to find wealthy interests to back him. In June 1863 he was finally forced to sell his California mining interests. Jessie was relieved that all of the problems relating to the mines were finally settled, and she busied herself with friends and charities.

The Civil War left the Frémonts disappointed, disillusioned, and distraught. They moved to upstate New York, to a home overlooking the Hudson River that they called Pocaho. Jessie was content to be out of the public eye; she wanted nothing more to do with political or military affairs. Retirement would be a welcome refuge, but there was one more battle to fight before such a respite could begin. The Frémonts, particularly John but with Jessie by his side, would confront their old nemesis Abraham Lincoln one more time.

In 1864, abolitionist factions attempted to mount a challenge

In May 1868, Jessie and her husband, along with 40,000 people, dedicated this bronze statue in honor of Sen. Thomas Hart Benton in Lafayette Park, St. Louis. In the figure's right hand is a rolled-up map representing Benton's lifelong commitment to westward expansion and American development. Many Missouri notables participated in the event, including an old political foe of the Frémonts—Frank Blair, Jr. His presence did not dampen the joy Jessie felt that day. She fondly recalled in *Souvenirs* that "when the speaker of the day dwelt on the public schools, and homestead laws, which had been cherished measures of my father's, who felt for all children, women, and helpless people, all knew he deserved the words of praise given him." (*Memoirs of My Life*, James S. Copley Library)

to the president's reelection, and Frémont was a logical and willing contender. In *Lincoln*, David Herbert Donald explains: "John C. Frémont had backers . . . both because he was known to hate Lincoln and because he had substantial support among the Germans and the Radicals, especially in Missouri." At a convention in Cleveland, Ohio, Frémont was promoted as a viable alternative to the president. Donald recounts:

> The only remaining obstacle to Lincoln's renomination was the convention of disaffected Republicans that assembled in Cleveland on May 31. Called to protest the "imbecile and vacillating policy of the present Administration in the conduct of the war," it initially seemed a real threat to Lincoln, who had agents on the ground to observe and report on the proceedings. But the gathering was poorly attended, with only 350-400 persons present, only 158 of whom were actual delegates. Most of these represented the German-American element, especially in Missouri, where hatred of Lincoln burned bright and loyalty to Frémont was fierce.

In the end, the convention did nominate Frémont for president, but his effort to confront Lincoln one more time failed. His candidacy did not attract numerous followers, and pressure was exerted upon him to withdraw from the race, which he eventually did. Now it was time to move on and Jessie looked forward to retirement. However, Frémont's lack of business acumen interfered with her plans.

In 1866, trying to capitalize on the need for transportation in the ever-expanding American West, Frémont became involved with a venture to build a transcontinental railroad, one with a southern route. The name of the company was the Memphis, El Paso, and Pacific Railroad. Seeking financial support for this project, Frémont traveled to Europe in June 1869, accompanied by Jessie. While they were in Paris, trouble developed. French backers misrepresented the company to potential supporters, saying that it had all of the necessary clearances to start building the railroad. In reality it did not.

Soon there were charges of bond fraud and calls for an investigation. Frémont, and, by association, Jessie, were caught in the middle of the scandal. Inquiries were conducted, both in France and by the Congress of the United States, and Frémont was cleared of any wrongdoing. Jessie was humiliated, though, and had to endure still another of her husband's failures. It was not to be the last time.

Shortly afterward, Frémont was caught up in yet another railroad scheme: an effort to rescue the holdings of the now bankrupt Memphis, El Paso, and Pacific Railroad. This project collapsed as well, and the failure was especially devastating to Jessie because Frémont had taken his financial machinations too far. This time it was more than a "paper loss"; the family lost their beloved Pocaho, their New York home. By 1873 they were left practically penniless.

To survive, to generate income, Jessie started writing again, about her life and the interesting experiences she had had. She wrote books and sold articles to the leading magazines of the day. Frémont, meanwhile, oversaw auctions and the sale of family treasures such as artwork, dishes, furniture, and books. They moved into cheaper housing to save money. Friends came to their aid, and in 1878 Frémont was appointed by President Rutherford B. Hayes to be the territorial governor of Arizona. The office came with a yearly salary of $2,000. Frémont gladly accepted the job, first because he needed the income, and second because he hoped to get involved in mining once more. And perhaps, just perhaps, this venture might restore some of his lost prestige.

Getting to Arizona was not easy, because no direct travel was available. Lily wrote in her *Recollections* that "the family was obliged to go first across the country to San Francisco, and thence to continue the trip to Arizona." They started for Prescott, the territorial capital, in September 1878. Lily described the journey as "a trip filled with many misgivings," almost as if they were traveling through "undiscovered country." The route from San Francisco to Los Angeles was over the Southern Pacific Railroad. All along the way, in the towns and hamlets where the

Prescott, Arizona, about the time Frémont was governor of the Arizona Territory. One of the few amenities that seem to have been available in this frontier town was a working brewery. (Arizona State Library, Archives and Public Records, Phoenix)

train stopped, the Frémonts were heartened by the reception they received from well-wishers. These greetings were a welcome relief from the hurtful feelings that lingered on the East Coast. In the West, Frémont was still a hero.

Once the Frémonts reached Yuma, Arizona, train travel ended and, Lily noted, they "started out for the rest of the journey in real pioneer fashion." They were met at Fort Yuma by a military escort of three army ambulances—small covered wagons—pulled by "six good mules in fine condition, and in charge of experienced drivers." They traveled 230 miles through the desert from Fort Yuma to Prescott. At night they pitched tents. Lily wrote that in the "early evening we found the softest places in the sand and there spread our blankets. Mother slept on the ambulance cushions, as became her custom, and thus enjoyed the one luxury of the trip. Father and the men slept outside the tent which was reserved for mother and me." The journey, which took eight days, was horrible: besides the oppressive heat, often there was no brush for firewood and little or no water to drink.

When they reached the outskirts of Prescott they were met by the outgoing governor, along with other public officials and their wives. The Frémonts rode into Prescott as conquering heroes—"a triumphal procession—the end of the journey reached," Lily wrote. Until they found their own housing, a member of the small Prescott community invited the Frémonts to stay in his home. This was typical of the "free handed hospitality of the far west." They enjoyed "a six-course dinner that first night," and were thrilled to find mail from home.

For a short term, the Frémonts rented a residence from a merchant who was leaving Prescott for a while. Eventually, Lily wrote, they "found a house that was built upon a hilltop, its walls made of solid planks unadorned, save by a covering of cotton sheeting." Before they moved in, their new quarters were given a through cleaning to rid it of pests and bugs that flourished in such dwellings.

Once settled, Jessie and Frémont began their new lives in Arizona. He occupied himself with governmental administrative duties and once more tried his hand at various mining schemes that he hoped would enrich him. Jessie became involved with the public school in Prescott. Teachers asked her, according to Lily, "to give the history class a talk every Friday during the school year, a task which she readily imposed upon her self and which she continued for ten months." In addition, Jessie found another interest when an order of Catholic nuns, the Sisters of St. Joseph, came to Prescott to establish a hospital. The nuns were from St. Louis, and Jessie was familiar with their work and eager to help them in any way she could.

Socially, the Frémonts engaged in whatever events there were, such as receptions, teas, and evening concerts performed by the army band. They did not have a luxurious life. The cost of living in a remote outpost such as Prescott was high. A $2,000 yearly salary did not go far, according to Lily:

The house rent was ninety dollars a month, and our Chinese cook was paid forty dollars a month for his services, so that there was little left for luxuries. The keeping of horses was an impossibility on that salary, hay selling for fifty dollars a ton. . . . [People] were compelled to pay nine dollars and fifty cents a cord for wood, twenty-five cents a can for the tomatoes and thirty cents a pound for the sugar.

Living in Arizona ultimately affected Jessie's health. Lily recalled: "Before our first year in the town drew to an end, the health of my mother was so seriously affected by the high altitude that she was sent home to New York. She soon recovered her old-time strength, though she never again ventured into Prescott." Frémont's health also became an issue—he suffered from "mountain fever," an infection spread by ticks. Hoping for better surroundings, he and Lily moved to Tucson in March 1881.

With Frémont in Arizona, Jessie lived in a small house on Staten Island in New York. Here she resumed her literary career, writing essays, articles, and books. Living frugally, she avoided the New York social scene, sending any extra money to Arizona. Again, Jessie and John had to live apart, but Frémont returned to New York as often as he could. Lily recorded one such trip when he went to New York on government business: to purchase guns and ammunition for Arizona because the Indians were becoming troublesome. While visiting with his family, Frémont tried to advance still another venture, this time involving a copper mine in which he had an interest. He could not find any investors, and his latest scheme to get rich quick was unsuccessful, just like all the others he had tried in the past.

Finally, in 1883 Frémont resigned as governor of the Arizona territory so he could return to New York and devote all of his time to his business plans, such as they were. During the 1870s and 1880s, Jessie was the prime wage earner, writing numerous stories and other pieces and becoming recognized as a fine chronicler of America's western past.

In 1888, a tree that Frémont used as his "headquarters" during his 1846 exploration of California was recognized and Frémont, Jessie, and Lily attended the festivities. (Frémont Letters and Papers, James S. Copley Library)

Shortly after Frémont returned to the East Coast, he and Jessie began one more project together, his *Memoirs of My Life*. Published in 1887, it was intended to be the first of two volumes. As it turned out, there would be no second volume, because Frémont became ill with pneumonia. Lily wrote that "his physician ordered him to Los Angeles. . . . [T]he physician was enthusiastic over the beneficial qualities of the climate of Southern California." Once more, and for the last time, Jessie and John went west.

Settling in the West was a good experience, because Frémont and Jessie were still celebrated figures there. They arrived in Los Angeles on December 24, 1887. Housing, as it always seemed to be in California, was again a problem, and for several months they lived in a hotel. Soon, Lily wrote, they "secured the well kept home of army friends who were leaving." Despite Jessie's literary success, money was still an issue, especially since Frémont was not eligible for a military pension. When the Civil War ended, he had resigned from the army, leaving behind his rank of major general and with it any retirement compensation he was entitled to receive.

In 1889 Frémont returned to New York, supposedly to attend to some business affairs. His real purpose was to try to have his military pension reinstated. Allan Nevins, in his biography of Frémont, explains: "[H]e had been deeply touched and gratified when his friends (prompted, it must be confessed, by Jessie) set on foot a movement to have him restored to the Army as a major-general, and placed on the retired list with pay, and he now gave them every assistance that was proper." The American people supported such a move, and in April 1890 Frémont was restored to the army payroll, slated to receive a retirement income suitable to the rank of major general—$6,000 a year. For the first time in a long time, he and Jessie would be financially stable. It looked as if they could have a nice retirement after all, but their good fortune did not last long.

After a strenuous day of activity in New York City, Frémont became ill with what we today would call food poisoning. Then it was called ptomaine poisoning; it developed into peritonitis. He was sick for two days and died on July 13, 1890. He was seventy-seven years old. His eldest son and namesake, John Charles Frémont, Jr., or Charley as he was known, an officer in the U.S. Navy, could be reached and was with his father when he died. Unfortunately, in an age when instant communication was in its infancy, Jessie could not be forewarned of her husband's illness. Lily wrote:

> My mother and I knew nothing of his illness until the news of his death was telegraphed to us. My mother was very ill for some time afterwards, and one of the very hard things to bear in those first days following his death was the daily arrival of his letters, filled with his plans and hopes for the future and for our lives in Los Angeles.

Friends gathered around us and did all that loving sympathy could do to help my mother bear her loss. She had known my father before she was sixteen and their lives were as one, to the end.

Frémont was buried in upstate New York, in a cemetery near the home he and Jessie once called Pocaho. There was not enough time for Jessie to travel the three thousand miles east for her husband's funeral and burial, but she asked Charley, via telegraph, to place her portrait in Frémont's hands—a small comfort to her. She had been married forty-nine years; the only person to whom she had been closer was her father. What would happen to Jessie now? How would she survive? Would the strength that she had displayed throughout her life carry her through this difficult time?

CHAPTER 10

Jessie Alone

*J*essie grieved over her husband's death for many months. They had been together for nearly fifty years, fought so many battles, collaborated on so many projects, and agreed on so many issues that at times it seemed, as Lily wrote, as if they were one. Now Jessie was alone. Eventually she moved on, but throughout the twelve years she lived without Frémont, he remained the center of her world and she continued to be the chief guardian of his memory.

One example of the many times in her remaining years that she protected the legacy of "the General" came almost immediately after his death. Frémont had been working on an article about California for *Century*, a leading magazine, and it fell to a distraught Jessie to finish the story. When one of the editors had the temerity, in Jessie's judgment, to suggest that some of Frémont's wording might need improving, Jessie shot back, staunchly defending her husband in a letter: "But there is not a fact—I think not even a wording that can be altered without injury to the whole. And the whole is the *final speaking* of the General. . . . I ask this for justice to the General. And for consolation to me." In the end, the article appeared with some minor changes that Jessie approved. From this point on, it became her mission to protect and promote her husband's place in history.

To that end, Jessie contemplated completing Frémont's memoirs, which originally were to be in two volumes. She also planned to work on her autobiography. Her ambitions, however,

Above, a self-portrait drawn by Jessie in 1901 from an 1899 photo, left. The sketch was made for a magazine that had asked for a picture of her to accompany an article she was writing. The caption reads: "I am 77 but do not look it. I [was] only 75 when that was made." (Frémont Letters and Papers, James S. Copley Library)

An 1890 photograph of the Los Angeles house that was presented to
Jessie and Lily by the California Federation of Women's Clubs. (Frémont
Letters and Papers, James S. Copley Library)

got ahead of her and neither project was ever completed. Jessie
did continue to write stories for prominent American magazines,
though, because it was a way to promote Frémont and because
she needed the income.

Often during her married life money was an issue. Nothing
changed with Frémont's death except, perhaps, that the situation worsened. Frémont died just after having his military retirement pension reinstated. With his passing, the yearly $6,000
payment ceased. Jessie now had no guaranteed income. Her son
Charley, who handled the final arrangements, quickly found out
as he settled Frémont's affairs that his father had left behind a lot
of debt. The news spread in the nation's newspapers that Jessie
had financial problems. Embarrassed by the notoreity over their
mother's finances, Jessie's sons, Charley and Frank, announced
that they would provide for her, yet Congress quickly voted to
give her an annual pension of $2,000. This annuity was not
enough to support her, though, and she did not want to be

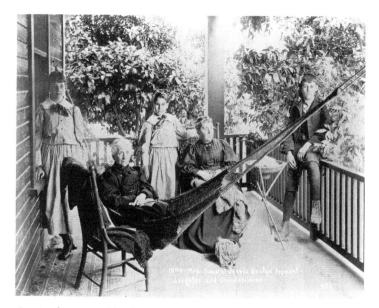

Jessie, her son Charley's children, and Lily enjoy the veranda of her home in Los Angeles in 1894. Dignitaries such as President William McKinley and Secretary of State John Hay also visited Jessie on her front porch. (Huntington Library)

beholden to her sons, so Jessie still wanted to earn a living. Hence, her stories for well-known publications became a necessity. She also needed an affordable place to live.

The women of Los Angeles came to her rescue. Jessie was on the fringe of the burgeoning women's movement. She was a friend of many of the leaders in the California Federation of Women's Clubs, but she never became an active participant in that organization. Perhaps the reason for this was that she was too busy defending her husband, or was too involved with her writing. Perhaps she did not agree with all of the movement's ideas or tactics, or just wanted to avoid the glare of public life. None of this mattered, because those in the movement were eager to embrace Jessie, and when it became known that she needed housing, the California women acted. They raised thousands of dollars, purchased a lot, and had a house built for Jessie

Seated at her desk in her California home, Jessie is surrounded by many mementos, including portraits of herself and her husband. (Bancroft Library)

and her daughter. In her book *Recollections*, Lily recorded her
mother's joy: "Her life [was] one of peaceful ease amid delightful
surroundings and dear friends. She often said that the climate of
California was delightful and a daily comfort to her, but better
far was that atmosphere of affectionate friendship which encom-
passed her."

By the mid-1890s Jessie's life had settled into a comfortable
pattern. Finally, she seemed to reach contentment in her life.
She and Lily had a wide circle of friends. At times family members visited. Jessie continued her writing and her limited association with California women who were promoting social issues.
One cause that interested her was early childhood education—
kindergarten. She was very aware of the work of Susan Blow, a
Missourian and innovator in schooling for young children. Jessie
wrote a friend: "I am proud of St. Louis when I remember its
noble advance work in education, *progressive* education, not
building on neglect but on wise and gentle care. Over the first of

the public schools is cut, in great stone letters, 'Benton School'—in memory of my Father's earnest work for education."

Jessie suffered the usual ailments that accompany aging, such as loss of hearing and arthritis, and in June 1900 she fell and fractured her left hip. Lily wrote of her life after this accident: "Though those two remaining years of her life were spent either in bed or in a rolling chair, she was always patient and cheerful, and to the last interested in the affairs of her friends and in the news of the world at large." Often Jessie spent part of her day on the porch of her house, watching as people passed by. For the woman who had traveled the globe, seen and visited unusual places, the world had now shrunk to the area of her veranda.

As 1902 neared its end, Jessie became more frail. On Christmas Eve her condition deteriorated, and on December 27, 1902, Jessie Benton Frémont died in her sleep. She was seventy-eight. An obituary in the *Los Angeles Times* the next day described the end of her life: "Up to Christmas morning Mme. Frémont retained her usual strength, but then she suddenly grew more feeble and before night relapsed into unconsciousness, from which she did not rally. The end was very peaceful."

The funeral was held on December 30. Neither of Jessie's sons attended. Charley, a naval officer, was in Washington, and Frank was in the army, stationed in Manila, the Philippines. Lily was there, along with one of Charley's children. Other mourners overflowed the church, according to newspaper accounts. Following the service there was a cremation, in accordance with Jessie's wishes. Later, her ashes were placed beside her husband in the Rockland Cemetery overlooking the Hudson River. The girl who was born in Virginia, spent her youth in St. Louis and Washington, D.C., crossed the Panamanian isthmus and visited European capitals, influenced the manifest destiny of America, met with and knew many influential people; debated important issues with the president of the United States, and who, as a transplanted Missourian, became a famed California citizen finally came to rest in New York. Her days of wandering were over.

Making History

Jessie Ann Benton Frémont was intelligent, educated, decisive, and bold. She was devoted to her family, especially her father and her husband. In fact, she was earnestly faithful, passionately loyal, and vehemently protective of her husband, John Charles Frémont, both during his life and after his death. All of these traits and characteristics led her to take actions that were not always believed suitable or correct for anyone, certainly not a woman.

She started her life with an independent streak fostered by her father, Thomas Hart Benton. From almost the time she was born, she was his favorite. He gave her unusual guidance, paying special attention to her education and providing her with opportunities that most children never have—including spending time in the Library of Congress and meeting important and influential people, including the president of the United States. These experiences allowed Jessie to develop a strong personality and a sense of purpose that she would have all of her life. Those qualities often got her into trouble, yet they provided her with the strength to face the many challenges that came her way.

Her adulthood began with the opposition of her parents to the man she married—not particularly significant by today's standards, but not insignificant for a nineteenth-century bride. Jessie's freethinking temperament caused the Bentons anxiety when she defied their wishes by eloping with a man of dubious parental and social background. For her, the choice of a husband was more than choosing a soul mate—she fell in love with a man

At her Los Angeles home, a nurse attends to Jessie on her porch. After she broke her hip in 1900, Jessie needed a wicker "rolling chair," as she called it, to get around. (Beale Memorial Library, Kern County Library, Bakersfield, California)

who so charmed her that she believed he would accomplish much and that together they would have a life of prominence and ease, similar to that of her parents. She was wrong.

At times, Jessie found herself in the middle of prickly situations that led her to act in an impetuous manner that was not consistent with the expected behavior of a woman in the nineteenth century. For example, when Frémont trekked west in 1843 and without proper authorization took a howitzer cannon with him, it was Jessie who managed to allow Frémont to continue his journey; it was Jessie's calculating intervention that saved her husband's expedition and possibly his career. In 1858, when it looked as if Frémont might lose a California gold mine to claim jumpers, it was Jessie who took charge and turned the situation in her husband's favor. Perhaps the most significant example of Jessie's protection of her husband came in 1861 with Frémont's challenge to the president over the issue of emancipation of slaves in Missouri. Instead of confronting Lincoln him-self, Frémont dispatched Jessie to Washington to do battle for him. This was an unusual act for any time, any age, any era—a military officer does *not* send his wife to his commander-in-chief to demand that his action be approved. But Frémont sent Jessie. He turned out not to be the achiever that she hoped he would be, but she always was his chief advocate nevertheless.

Jessie showed her tenacity in other ways, too. When the Frémonts faced financial difficulties, it was she who came to the rescue. With her husband's businesses taking a steep downward turn and the family income declining, Jessie began her literary career. She wrote about all the unique and extraordinary experi-ences she had had during her life. Her articles appeared in lead-ing magazines; her books detailed the people, places, and events she had encountered; and she worked on Frémont's memoirs. Jessie did this while Frémont liquidated family assets and launched potential moneymaking schemes. Once more, Jessie was the steady one, the one who dealt with reality. She was com-ing out, ever so slightly, from the long shadow cast by her father and husband. She would never completely emerge from the effect of their celebrity, but she did make a name for herself. The strength she learned as a child served her well.

Nothing Jessie did was deemed proper for a woman of her era. Not many women or men of that time made trips across the isthmus of Panama to California as she did in 1849. It was diffi-cult, but Jessie did it. She had made a decision early on to become the partner of John Charles Frémont. At the time it seemed the exciting thing to do, because, in part, he shared the same ideas she learned from her father. She, too, came to embrace those dreams, and she looked to Frémont to succeed in fulfilling them. With him, she believed, her life would be one of adven-ture and success. The only part of the dream that came true, however, was that she led an adventurous life. Although she did earn stature and fame, traditional success, as defined by the period she lived in, eluded her. Yet she never regretted the deci-sion she made as a sixteen-year-old. Her life might not have been the one she planned, but it was unique.

A typical upper-class nineteenth-century household included slaves, servants—black, white, or indentured—cooks, seamstresses, blacksmiths, carriage drivers, tutors, and other help. Often Jessie had none of these. She camped in tents, slept in a carriage, lived on the deck of a ship, rode a mule across steep mountain trails, and traveled in a whaleboat and covered wagons. She did at times live in a proper home and stay in hotels and fine European accommodations. Taken as a whole, however, her life was anything but conventional, in any era. She irritated some; she was a heroine to others; she participated in political and social events; she chronicled her life and those of her father and husband; she protected the man she loved, during his life and until she herself died. Jessie was a symbol of all that was good about her Missouri roots, and as one of the founders of California she was foremost among those from Missouri who settled in that state.

Jessie was a part of many changes in America's history and witnessed many more. During its manifest destiny era, the country expanded across the continent to the Pacific Ocean, allowing nothing to stand in its way—not nations, not treaties, not people, not mountains, not rivers, not any obstacle. It was also a time of tremendous political upheaval. It was a time of civil war, when brother fought against brother, father against son, and so many lives were lost. It was a time of great social turmoil, when emancipation finally came to slaves and when citizenship was finally imparted to them, along with the right to vote. It was a time when women rallied to secure long-sought universal and political social equality.

These were turbulent and exciting happenings that Jessie observed. The important fact to remember is that all of these events were made or caused by the actions of men, not women. But because Jessie was not a traditional nineteenth-century woman, she showed those of her era, as well as those that followed, what it truly means to make a difference. She herself best summarized her life when she wrote in her introduction to her

This portrait of Jessie, painted in 1856 by T. Buchanan Read, hung in the Frémont home for years. Jessie's daughter, Lily, donated it on August 20, 1914, to the Southwest Museum, the oldest museum in Los Angeles, founded in 1907. *(Memoirs of My Life,* James S. Copley Library, and the Autry National Center of the Southwest Museum, Braun Research Library, Los Angeles)

husband's book: "By family I belonged to all that was old and fixed in the South and yet . . . I left home, family, friends and political affiliations, to join General Frémont in his choice of principles over self-interest." For good or ill, Jessie embraced those beliefs and made them her own. She was not always right, but she was steadfast in her determination—some would say headstrong. Nonetheless, she made her own record and her own impression on America, entwined though it might be with her family's story. "Well-behaved women seldom make history," the historian Laurel Thatcher Ulrich once observed. Jessie Ann Benton Frémont made history.

For More Reading

Research for this book led to a variety of sources: some materials related directly to Jessie and others described the historical period in which she lived. Selected for the reader's consideration are only a portion of the narratives studied, and we hope they are listed in a way that will be helpful to those who are interested in learning more about Jessie and her times. Obviously, the most highly recommended sources are those that Jessie wrote herself. She had a vast knowledge not only of the events she was a part of but also of the place those events had in history and thus of her place in history as well. Most of the accounts listed here meet a certain criteria: accessibility. With the exception of the information found only at the James S. Copley Library in La Jolla, California; the Bancroft Library at the University of California, Berkeley; and the Huntington Library in San Marino, California, these books should be available in all large academic libraries.

Primary Sources

WORKS BY JESSIE BENTON FRÉMONT

Far-West Sketches (Boston: D. Lothrop, 1890).
Introduction to *Memoirs of My Life,* by John Charles Frémont (Chicago: Belford, Clarke, 1887).
Letters and Papers of Jessie Benton Frémont, James S. Copley Library, La Jolla, California.
"The Origin of the Frémont Explorations," *Century Magazine,*

March 1891, pp. 766–71.

Souvenirs of My Time (Boston: D. Lothrop, 1887).

The Story of the Guard: A Chronicle of the War (Boston: Ticknor and Fields, 1863).

The Will and the Way Stories (Boston: D. Lothrop, 1891).

A Year of American Travel (1878; reprint, San Francisco: Book Club of California, 1960).

WORKS BY JOHN CHARLES FRÉMONT

The Expeditions of John Charles Frémont, 3 vols., edited by Donald Jackson and Mary Lee Spence (Urbana: University of Illinois Press, 1970–1984).

Letters and Papers of John Charles Frémont, James S. Copley Library, La Jolla, California.

Memoirs of My Life (1887; reprint, New York: Cooper Square Press, 2001).

"Proclamation of General John C. Frémont," St. Louis, Missouri, August 31, 1861. http://www.sonofthesouth.net/leefoundation/civil-war/1861/september/slave-proclamation.html

ADDITIONAL PRIMARY SOURCES

Attention, Pioneers! Facsimile Reproductions of Twelve Rare California Broadsides or Posters, from the Collection of Carl I. Wheat. San Francisco: Book Club of California, 1952.

Frémont Family Papers. Bancroft Library, University of California, Berkeley.

Funeral Sermon for Mrs. Thomas Hart Benton, by Rev. Nathan Lewis Rice, Second Presbyterian Church, St. Louis, March 26, 1855. Missouri Historical Society, St. Louis.

"General Frémont Dead." *New York Tribune*, July 14, 1890.

"Gen. Frémont's Widow Dead." *New York Times*, December 29, 1902.

"Notice" [reward offer for Kit Carson], *Missouri Intelligencer*, October 12, 1826.

"Pathfinder's Widow Crosses the Divide." *Los Angeles Times*, December 28, 1902.

Recollections of Elizabeth Benton Frémont, compiled by I. T. Martin (New York: Frederick H. Hitchcock, 1912).

Rocky Mountain Song Book. 1856. James S. Copley Library, La Jolla, California.

Song Book for the Campaign of 1856. (Indianapolis, Ind.: M'Clure and Hand, 1856).

Thirty Years' View; or, a History of the Working of the American Government from 1820 to 1850, by Thomas Hart Benton, 2 vols. (New York: D. Appleton, 1854–1856).

"To Help Frémont's Daughter." *New York Times*, January 30, 1900.

Secondary Sources

Abraham Lincoln: A History, by John G. Nicolay and John Hay, 10 vols. (New York: Century Co., 1904), a lengthy history by Lincoln's secretaries that includes details of pre–Civil War conditions in Missouri and provides wonderful insight into Lincoln's association with both Jessie and her husband.

Abraham Lincoln: The War Years, by Carl Sandburg, 4 vols. (New York: Harcourt, Brace, 1939), won its author the Pulitzer Prize in history.

Agriculture and Slavery in Missouri's Little Dixie, by R. Douglas Hurt (Columbia: University of Missouri Press, 1992), details the economy in mid-Missouri in the years preceding the Civil War.

California in the Fifties, by Douglas S. Watson (San Francisco: John Howell, 1936), conveys through vivid pictures and sketches a sense of what the early towns and cities of California looked like.

The Chagres: River of Westward Passage, by John Easter Minter

(New York: Rinehart, 1948), a fascinating book on the difficult journey of crossing the Panamanian isthmus as one way to get to the West Coast. This book nicely complements Jessie's own account of traveling to California, *A Year of American Travel*.

Cities of the American West, by John W. Reps (Princeton, N.J.: Princeton University Press, 1979), includes interesting drawings of settlements and towns of the early West.

Dictionary of Missouri Biography, edited by Lawrence O. Christensen, William F. Foley, Gary R. Kremer, and Kenneth H. Winn (Columbia: University of Missouri Press, 1999), a collection of brief, reliable biographies of famous Missourians, including Jessie, her husband, and her father.

The Famous Fremonts and Their America, by Alice Eyre (Los Angeles: Fine Arts Press, 1948), another assessment of Jessie and her husband and their influence on America and their times.

Frank Blair: Lincoln's Conservative, by William E. Parrish (Columbia: University of Missouri Press, 1998), provides background on the Blair-Frémont feud as well as historical information about Missouri, Lincoln, and the Civil War.

Frémont: Pathmarker of the West, by Allan Nevins (New York: Longmans, Green, 1955), a biography of John Charles Frémont, gives a broad overview of his life, with many details about Jessie.

Gray Ghosts of the Confederacy: Guerrilla Warfare in the West, 1861–1865, by Richard S. Brownlee (Baton Rouge: Louisiana State University Press, 1958), is a clear, well-written study of a different aspect of the Civil War: the vicious guerrilla campaigns that were waged by Confederate supporters to further their cause.

History of California: Vol. 6, 1848–1859, by Hubert Howe Bancroft, vol. 23 of *The Works of Hubert Howe Bancroft* (San Francisco: A. L. Bancroft, 1888), a general nineteenth-century history of California that is still a good source of contemporaneous information.

Immortal Wife: The Biographical Novel of Jessie Benton Frémont, by Irving Stone (New York: Doubleday, Doran, 1944), is a work of historical fiction, blending actual events with imagined conversations, that unfortunately has found its way into the history of America as fact.

Inside War: The Guerrilla Conflict in Missouri during the American Civil War, by Michael Fellman (New York: Oxford University Press, 1989), gives Civil War enthusiasts a complete account of all things political and military regarding the internal upheaval that gripped Missouri.

Jessie Benton Frémont: A Biography, by Pamela Herr (New York: Franklin Watts, 1987), is the most recent full-length biography of Jessie.

Jessie Benton Frémont: A Woman Who Made History, by Catherine Coffin Phillips (San Francisco: John Henry Nash, 1935), an earlier biography of Jessie, provides insight into Jessie's childhood and the events that influenced her.

Kit Carson Days, by Edwin L. Sabin (New York: Press of the Pioneers, 1935), assesses the well-known adventurer and the part he played in the development of the American West.

"A Letter from Jessie to Kit," ed. Janet Lecompte (*Missouri Historical Society Bulletin* 29 [1973]: 260–63), highlights the close friendship that Jessie and Kit Carson shared. Of particular interest is the frankness that Kit demonstrated to Jessie when her son Benton was born.

The Letters of Jessie Benton Frémont, edited by Pamela Herr and Mary Lee Spence (Urbana: University of Illinois Press, 1993), is an important book given the fact that a fire at the Benton home in 1855 destroyed many items, including correspondence.

Lincoln, by David Herbert Donald (New York: Simon and Schuster, 1995), an informative and well-written biography by the two-time Pulitzer Prize–winning author. The generous use of Lincoln's own words helps to make this book of great value to anyone interested in reading and learning about one of America's foremost citizens.

The Men of the California Bear Flag Revolt and Their Heritage, by Barbara R. Warner (Sonoma, Calif.: Arthur H. Clark, 1996), details the origin and evolution of the California flag.

Missouri: Heart of the Nation, by William E. Parrish, Charles T. Jones, Jr., and Lawrence O. Christensen (Wheeling, Ill.: Harlan Davidson, 1980, 1992), provides all that is needed for those who want a good overview of the history of Missouri.

"The Myth of the Frémont Howitzer," by Donald Jackson (*Missouri Historical Society Bulletin* 23 [1966–1967]: 205–14), an interesting piece of historical research in which the author takes on the controversy over the roles played by Jessie, Frémont, and Benton in the cannon escapade.

Notes of a Voyage to California via Cape Horn, by Samuel C. Upham (Philadelphia: privately printed, 1878), a narrative of a passage to the California gold fields and a good source of information on how events unfolded during that time period.

Old Bullion Benton: Senator from the West, by William Nisbet Chambers (Boston: Little, Brown, 1956), focuses on Thomas Hart Benton's political contributions to the emerging American manifest destiny movement.

Trail to California: The Overland Journal of Vincent Geiger and Wakeman Bryarly, edited by David Morris Potter (New Haven, Conn.: Yale University Press, 1945), is a most helpful document that compares and contrasts the various means of travel for getting to California during the years of the gold rush.

Up and Down California in 1860–1864: The Journal of William H. Brewer, edited by Francis P. Farquhar (New Haven, Conn.: Yale University Press, 1930), is another account of what life was like in early California.

"Vertuous Women Found: New England Ministerial Literature, 1668–1735," by Laurel Thatcher Ulrich (*American Quarterly* 28 [1976]: 20–40), makes the interesting argument that women who follow custom and tradition seldom make a mark on the times in which they live.

The White House Gallery of Official Portraits of the Presidents

(New York and Washington: Gravure Company of America, 1901), contains pictures of all U.S. presidents until the date of its publication.

GOVERNMENT PUBLICATIONS

Report of the Exploring Expedition to the Rocky Mountains, by John Charles Frémont, United States Government, March 1843. One of the many Frémont reports, all of which Jessie helped to write, this essay tells of his experiences on a trip to the American frontier in 1842, the one on which Jessie's brother accompanied him for part of the way.

State of Missouri. *An Ordinance Abolishing Slavery in Missouri*. January 1865. This document immediately ended slavery in Missouri months before national emancipation took effect.

United States of America. *The Emancipation Proclamation*. September 1862. Delineates Lincoln's effort to abolish slavery in the United States during the Civil War.

United States of America. Twenty-eighth Congress, Senate, 2nd session, *Report of the Exploring Expedition to the Rocky Mountains*, by John Charles Frémont, 1843. Official government record of Frémont's 1842 trek to the west.

ONLINE SITES

Various Web sites on the Internet have information about Jessie, her husband, her father, and subjects related to them. There are too many to mention, but any search engine can be of help.

Index

Page numbers in bold refer to illustrations or captions.

About the Authors

Ilene Stone is a former adjunct faculty member in American history at San Diego Community College, where she taught for more than thirty years. She is the author of *Jane Froman: Missouri's First Lady of Song* (University of Missouri Press).

Suzanna M. Grenz is Associate Professor of American History at Palomar College in San Marcos, California.